NEW
PROFICIENCY
ENGLISH

BOOK THREE

Use of English

NEW PROFICIENCY ENGLISH

BOOK THREE

Use of English

W. S. Fowler

Nelson

Thomas Nelson and Sons Ltd
Nelson House   Mayfield Road
Walton-on-Thames   Surrey
KT12 5PL   UK

51 York Place
Edinburgh
EH1 3JD   UK

Thomas Nelson (Hong Kong) Ltd
Toppan Building 10/F
22A Westlands Road
Quarry Bay   Hong Kong

Designed by The New Book Factory
Printed in Hong Kong

Contents

Introduction

New Proficiency English

New Proficiency English is planned as a replacement of *Proficiency English*, published in 1976–8, and as a logical continuation of *New First Certificate English*, published in 1984. In effect, it is the result of several years' experience of using the previous course and gradually adapting materials to the needs of students taught at earlier stages in the learning process by different methods from those current in the early 1970s. As in the case of *New First Certificate English*, my co-authors, John Pidcock and Robin Rycroft, and I have preferred to write a new course, taking this experience into account, rather than to revise the original. While some elements that have proved particularly successful have been retained – above all in *Book 3*, Use of English, where the revised Cambridge syllabus of 1984 for the paper shows no innovations – over 80% of the material in the course is new.

By this time, it will be evident that the examination as such has not changed to a noticeable extent either in level of difficulty or in form, except in the design of the aural/oral tests (covered in this course in *Book 4*). The main change in approach, especially in *Book 1*, has therefore been to shift the emphasis away from the formal presentation of grammar towards the acquisition of skills. At the same time, the overall coverage remains the same.

The main problem for teachers at advanced level and for students attempting the Proficiency examination is that the former are inclined to relax the pressure once students have passed First Certificate because the Proficiency examination is still a long way away, while the latter underestimate the difference in standard. This course has been written for students likely to attempt the examination two years after First Certificate if they attend classes five hours a week (300 hours) or three years after if they attend three hours a week (270 hours). The material has been pretested and graded through use with students at each stage to allow for the time-span envisaged, but it is above all important to point out that the language–learning process should be continuous. Our experience leads us to believe that it is necessary to develop skills methodically throughout the period and that it is unwise to imagine that students can be left largely to their own devices for a year or so before making a systematic approach to the examination.

The design of the course

The four books comprising the new course can be used independently in order to concentrate on a specific paper in the examination, but they have been written in such a way that they relate to each other. *Book 3* is related to *Book 1* in two ways. The first section contains structural revision exercises. Each exercise carries a number in square brackets which is that of the corresponding unit in *Book 1*, as well as a reference number of its own. These exercises are planned to provide practice of structures likely to be required by students in specific compositions and are to be used whenever the teacher has reason to believe that revision is necessary. The passages for comprehension and summary (Section 2) and the selective cloze exercises which in part derive from them (Section 5) are thematically linked to corresponding units in *Book 1* in most cases so that students are able to concentrate more fully on the content and the grammatical problems raised respectively, without being inhibited by lexical difficulties. In all cases, structures have been presented so as to coincide with the grading of *Book 1*, and the best results will be obtained by using the books in conjunction, following the chart on page 7 of this book and the advice given in the *Teacher's Guide*.

Types of exercises

The new Use of English paper for the Proficiency examination retains two of its original sections, the first testing knowledge of usage in a variety of ways, the second consisting of a passage followed by direct questions, which must also be summarised; the third section, guided composition, has been transferred to the Composition paper, and is therefore covered in *Book 1* of this course.

This book is divided into five teaching sections, the first containing structural revision exercises, already referred to above, the second consisting of passages for comprehension and summary, and the remainder devoted to usage. The order of the sections is deliberate, based on the most effective order discovered during pretesting of the material. It must be emphasised that students should work through the book, completing all the exercises for Unit 1 (indicated in brackets [1]), irrespective of section heading, before going on to those for Unit 2. In other words, the chart on page 7 should be followed *horizontally*, rather than vertically. The index on page 122 can be used at any time to provide practice of any specific grammatical point.

Structural revision

The purpose of this section is, as explained above, to provide practice of structures likely to be required by students in order to write specific compositions. At the same time, I have made use of the research undertaken to establish the main grammatical problems of advanced students and the degree of difficulty involved in each case which went in to the composition of *Practise Your English Book 3* (Fowler and Coe, 1983), and in some cases have reprinted exercises from that book. In this way, particularly for the benefit of students attempting the Proficiency examination over a long period of time, structures have been designated as appropriate for revision at different stages, according to difficulty and frequency of occurrence in good, modern English. As a result, there are comparatively fewer exercises from Unit 17 onwards, where the examination year would begin in three-year courses. By that time, only the more esoteric structures favoured by Cambridge examiners, such as inversion, which are of little practical value in the production of language, remain to be dealt with.

Passages for comprehension and summary

This section of the book is the part of the course that most closely resembles the original in *Proficiency English Book 3* (1978). The passages have proved eminently suitable for their purpose over the past few years and I have therefore retained most of them. I have, however, considerably expanded the advice given to students on answering questions and writing summaries. Students should pay particular attention to the presentation of summary techniques on page 40 and to subsequent advice in later units.

Structural conversion

This section covers the second group of questions in the examination, and is by its nature the most mechanical. The order in which the exercises appear follows the order of structural requirements for composition work in *Book 1*. The exercises themselves will be of most use if they are treated not merely as a means to an end from an examination point of view, but also as a genuine attempt to develop students' means of expression by offering an alternative way of saying something. In cases where I consider the alternative structure to be of little practical value and it has only been included

because it has frequently appeared as an examination item, I have made this plain. Five progress tests are included, one after every four units, incorporating all the main points raised in previous exercises. These have been fully pretested, and the results are given in the *Teacher's Guide*. The last four units each contain a general revision exercise of the same kind.

Rephrasing

In this section, I have attempted to deal with the questions in the examination that ask students either to complete sentences with appropriate phrases or to rewrite them, using a given word. Many of these questions require a knowledge of phrasal verbs, a source both of fascination and of frustration for the majority of advanced students. Phrasal verbs can seldom be found in sufficient numbers in modern prose to be taught except as they occur, in isolation. I have therefore included exercises grouping them under main verbs in which students are asked to substitute the correct verb plus preposition for a paraphrase; in this way, they are helped towards recognition of the meaning and context of the phrasal verb. The other types of exercise are exemplified at the beginning of Section 4 but the exercises are not always in examination format at first since in many cases examination items require the student to read the examiner's mind in order to decide on the correct answer. I have therefore prepared for this kind of question gradually, only adopting the examination format in the closing units of the book. This group of exercises, rephrasing by using a given word, is likely to be the most interesting for students, and time should be found for them for that reason; it cannot be pretended, however, that every conceivable variation open to the examiners can be covered. A group of exercises that I regard as essential, on the other hand, within this section, is that on comparative verb structure, where the variations presented with common verbs are of great importance to students' own production of language.

Selective cloze

This section deals with the first question in the examination paper, but for classroom purposes is best dealt with last. The gaps to be filled are in many cases a recapitulation of structural points presented in other exercises relating to the same unit, and to a certain extent the paragraphs reflect the themes of the unit in *Book 1*; in all units where there is a summary to be completed, the paragraph containing selective cloze paraphrases part of the original passage. Students unfamiliar with this kind of exercise can easily score low marks because they do not take the trouble to work out the overall meaning of the passage before beginning to answer. I have therefore included detailed guidance on the most sensible approaches at the beginning of the section.

Test papers

There are three test papers in the Cambridge format at the end of the book. They have been thoroughly pretested, and full details of the pretesting appear in the *Teacher's Guide*. I am grateful to the 500 students who took part in the pretesting, which was carried out in two schools in Barcelona with above-average pass levels in the Proficiency examination.

Appendix

The appendix of verbs and prepositions, in common with other reference sections within the course, is intended to provide students with a constant source of information when they are working at home, as they should do if they hope to pass the examination.

> Will Fowler,
> Barcelona, August 1984

Acknowledgements

I am very grateful to Simon Clackson, English Language Officer, Barcelona, Sheila Hennessey, Assistant Director of Studies, The British Council Institute, Barcelona, and Peter Clements, Director, the CIC, Barcelona, for permission to pretest all the test materials in this book in their schools. I would also like to thank all the teachers and students who took part, and in particular Peter Goode and Ron Round for a number of useful suggestions.

The publishers wish to thank the following for permission to reproduce photographs:

Kobal Collection p 45; Camerapix Hutchison Library p 47; Barnaby's Picture Library pp 49, 56, 58; National Portrait Gallery p 59.

Photography (p 52) and photographic research, Terry Gross.

The author and the publishers are very grateful for permission to reproduce in this book extracts for the following articles:

'A Space in the Country' by Brian Jackman, first published in *The Sunday Times Magazine* 6 June 1976; 'Flagging Interest' by Brian Love, first published in *The Sunday Times Magazine* 11 January 1976 and later in *Penny Paper, Sixpenny Silk*; 'How Safe are British Dams?' and 'Cost and Compassion' by Fabian Acker and 'Chemical Threat to Lake Nakuru' by Dr Roger Lewin, which first appeared in *New Scientist* 10 February 1977, 22 July 1976 and 23 September 1976; 'The Counties: Middlesex' by James Bishop, reproduced by permission of *The Illustrated London News* Picture Library; 'Greenwich Newly Observed' by Tony Aldous and 'Liberty and Equality' by John Mackintosh, MP, first published in *The Illustrated London News*, March 1975 and February 1976; 'Constable's Country' © Edward Lucie-Smith 1977.

Correspondence Chart

The chart shows the relationship between the exercises in *Book 3* and the units in *Book 1*.

Book 1	Book 3 Section headings				
Unit	Structural revision	Passages for comprehension	Structural conversion	Rephrasing	Selective cloze
[1]	1,2,3,4		67,68,69	110,111	178,179
[2]	5,6,7,8,9		70,71,72,73	112,113,114	180
[3]	10,11,12,13	43,44	74,75,76,77,78	115,116	181
[4]	14	45,46	79,80,81,PT1	117,118,119	182
[5]	15,16,17,18,19		82	120,121,122	183
[6]	20		83,84,85	123,124	184
[7]	21	47,48	86,87	125,126,127	185
[8]	22	49,50	88,89,90,PT2	128,129,130	186
[9]	23,24		91	131,132,133	187
[10]	25,26,27,28		92	134,135,136	188
[11]	29,30,31	51,52	93,94,95	137,138	189
[12]		53,54	96,97,PT3	139,140	190
[13]	32,33			141,142	191
[14]	34,35,36		98	143,144,145	192
[15]		55,56		146,147	193
[16]		57,58	PT4	148,149,150	194
[17]	37,38,39		99	151,152,153,154	195
[18]			100,101	155,156,157	196
[19]	40,41,42	59,60	102,103	158,159,160	197
[20]		61,62	104,105,PT5	161,162,163	198.
[21]			106	164,165,166,167	199
[22]			107	168,169,170	200
[23]		63,64	108	171,172,173,174	201
[24]		65,66	109	175,176,177	202

PT = Progress Test

Section 1: Structural revision

[1] 1

Word order of adjectives

It is difficult to give clear rules to follow about the position of adjectives before the noun. The list below, however, should be of value as a useful check in given cases. The following general points should also be remembered.

1 We seldom use **and** except when the adjectives are a complement, following **be**:

*His work is untidy **and** unsatisfactory.*

2 We usually put the more or most precise adjective nearest the noun, but it is not always easy to decide which is more precise. When in doubt, consult the examples and order given below:

All the first three competitors broke the record. (1,2,3,4)
The beautiful intelligent girl fell in love with the tall young man. (2,5,6 and 2,7,8)
There was a round green spot on the carved wooden Japanese screen. (9,10 and 2,11,12,13)
He had a beautiful old ivory chess piece. (5,8,12,14)

1) **both, all** or **half**
2) **the**
3) Ordinal number (**first, last**)
4) Cardinal number (**one, three**)
5) General judgement (**good, bad, nice, beautiful**)
6) General judgement (mental – **intelligent, stupid**)
7) Measurement (**big, tall**)
8) Age or temperature (**old, young, hot**)
9) Shape (**round, square**)
10) Colour (**red, green**)
11) Verb participle form (**carved, boiling**)
12) Material (**wooden**)
13) Origin, nationality (**French, Mediterranean**)
14) Noun in apposition (**steel, cigarette**)

Some of these categories are reversed at times, particularly the following:

6 and 7 for emphasis on 6. In this case, the comma must always be used:
A little, intelligent man (7,6)

10 and 13 in a phrase like:
Yugoslavian white wine (13,10)

Here **white** is used to describe a type, in contrast to **red**, rather than as an indication of colour.

- Put the adjectives in brackets in what seems to you the most normal position and order in the sentences, and then compare your decision with the guidelines above.

1 She had a dress on. (bright, green)
2 A girl opened the door. (little, pretty)
3 She lives in a (an) house. (country, lovely, old)
4 He seems a (an) man. (intelligent, young)
5 Have you done the questions yet? (first, four)
6 A dog stood watching us. (big, black, great)
7 For his birthday, I bought him a chess set, with chessmen. (Indian, lovely) (ivory, carved)
8 His portrait didn't flatter him. The artist gave him a face and lips. (lined, long) (red, thick)
9 He's bought a car. (German, new, sports, yellow)
10 The game is played with a set of balls and a ball that you have to aim at (grooved, metal, round, three) (little, wooden)

[1] 2

Comparison

A   Comparative and superlative

Compare these sentences:

Peter Fonda is a good actor, but his sister, Jane, is more famous.
Groucho was probably the best known of the Marx Brothers.

He was one of the funniest men { *in the world.*
I've ever seen.

The comparative form is only used when the context indicates that there are only two alternatives; elsewhere, we use the superlative, as in the third example above where it is logical that there are more than two funny men.

- Put the adjectives given in brackets in the following passage into the correct form, comparative or superlative. Add **the** or **a**, where necessary.

9

One of (1 embarrassing) experiences that can happen to anyone is to meet old friends and not recognise them. I once had to welcome a group of students at the airport. I knew (2 old) person, a Madame Dufort, would be in charge of them, and when the group appeared, this woman came towards me, smiling, and said: 'David, what a pleasant surprise!' If I had been (3 quick) and (4 intelligent) I would have said brightly: 'How nice to see you, my dear!' as if she were my (5 old) friend, but I just stood there, my face getting (6 red) and (7 red), trying to remember her. The (8 bad) thing about it was that she got even (9 embarrassed) than I was, and said:'You don't remember me,' still not giving me (10 slight) clue. Fortunately, my wife, who is (11 quick-thinking) and (12 well-mannered) than I am, said: 'Of course he does, Nicole, but he's (13 absent-minded) person in the world.' Nicole had been a student of mine years before, but she looked much (14 old), her hair was going grey, and her face had (15 many) lines in it than is usual at her age. She had got married, too, so her name had changed, and I find names (16 easy) to remember than faces.

B Two-syllable adjectives: comparative and superlative

Notice the forms of the adjectives in these sentences:

*Angela is **more careless** than Susan in her work. She's **the most careless** person I know.*
*This exercise is **easier** than the others; in fact, it's **the easiest** one we've done so far.*

For the rules regarding usage in the formation of comparatives and superlatives from two-syllable adjectives, see the Reference Section of *Book 1*.

■ Complete these sentences with the correct form of the adjectives given in brackets.

1 I know the exams are the _____ time of year for you, but you ought to be _____ with the students. (busy, patient)
2 He was much the same as I had remembered him, though he had grown _____ and _____. But his hair was even _____ and he had a _____ expression. (heavy, thickset, curly, pleasant)
3 They were suspicious of us at first but eventually they became _____ and _____. (friendly, relaxed)
4 Considering everything you have done for them, they ought to be _____ and _____ to help. (grateful, willing)

5 He's one of the _____ people I have ever met. He parked his car in the _____ street in the village, and when another driver complained, he just got _____ and _____. In the end, a policeman came and fined him. Perhaps he'll be _____ in future. (stupid, narrow, angry, awkward, careful)

C the more . . . the more

Notice the form of the adjectives and adverbs in these sentences:

***The better** the horse, **the easier** it is to ride.*
***The more** you eat, **the fatter** you get.*
***The faster** you drive, **the more likely** you are to have an accident.*

When two things vary to the same extent, we use the comparative form in each part of the sentence, as in the examples above.

■ Put the adjectives and adverbs in brackets into the comparative form to complete the following sentences.

1 The _____ they come, the _____ they fall. (big, hard)
2 The _____ you are, the _____ you are to a heart attack. (fat, liable)
3 The _____ we control pollution, the _____ the environment will be. (much, clean)
4 The _____ the lecture went on, the _____ the students became. (long, sleepy)
5 The _____ he gets, the _____ he becomes. He suffers from rheumatism, and the trouble is that the _____ he does, the _____ it gets. (old, irritable, little, bad)
6 A The _____ they have to wait, the _____ they'll become, and the _____ they'll complain. (long, impatient, much)
   B I don't mind. The _____ they shout, the _____ I am to take any notice of them. (much, likely)

D The same (as), different (from), similar (to), like, alike, unlike

Study the following examples before attempting the exercise:

Our conclusions are the same, although our approach is { ***different.***
                                                              not the same.

He has reached the same conclusions as I have, although his study

$$\left\{\begin{array}{l} is \\ isn't \end{array}\right\} \text{based on} \left\{\begin{array}{l} \textbf{different} \\ \textbf{the same} \end{array}\right\} \text{evidence} \left\{\begin{array}{l} \textbf{from} \\ \textbf{as} \end{array}\right\} \text{mine.}$$

A He's $\left\{\begin{array}{l} \textbf{like} \\ \textbf{similar to} \end{array}\right\}$ *his father in many ways.*

B Yes, they're $\left\{\begin{array}{l} \textbf{alike.} \\ \textbf{similar.} \end{array}\right.$

A But he's $\left\{\begin{array}{l} \textbf{not like} \\ \textbf{different from} \end{array}\right\}$ *his mother.*

B True. They're $\left\{\begin{array}{l} \textbf{not alike.} \\ \textbf{different.} \end{array}\right.$

Like *his father, he's very patient.*
Unlike *his mother, he never loses his temper.*

■ Study the information given below about Bernard and James, who were born on the same day, but are not identical twins. Then make as many comparisons as you can, using the following forms:

a) Bernard and James are alike/similar because . . . the same . . .
b) James is like/similar to Bernard because he . . . the same . . . as . . .
c) Bernard and James are not alike/different in some ways because . . . different . . .
d) James is not like/different from Bernard because he . . . different . . . from . . . (not . . . the same . . . as . . .)
e) Like James, Bernard . . .
f) Unlike Bernard, James . . .

	Bernard	**James**
age	16	16
height	1 m 86	1 m 65
weight	72 kg	60 kg
colour eyes	blue	blue
colour hair	brown	brown
studies	Mathematics	Languages
interests	football, tennis	music, dancing, swimming
personality	serious, quiet, introvert	lively, friendly, talkative

[1] 3

Relative clauses: defining and non-defining

Defining
The man **who came into the shop** *was wearing a raincoat.*
The table **that stood in the corner** *was dirty.*
The girl **whose dog bit me** *just laughed.*

Defining relative clauses are essential to the meaning of the sentence. If we take out the relative clause from the examples above, we must ask the speaker for further information in order to understand the sentence, e.g., **Which man? Which table?** or **Which girl?**

Non-defining
My brother Jack, **who has just come back from Australia,** *plays the piano beautifully.*
My brother Jack – he's just come back from Australia, actually – plays the piano beautifully.
My brother Jack plays the piano beautifully. He's just come back from Australia

Non-defining relative clauses give additional information about a person or thing. They are seldom found in speech, where we prefer to use **and**, or make a parenthesis, or begin a new sentence.

A Non-defining relative clauses

Look at the forms used to make non-defining relative clauses before doing the exercise:

She married **my uncle Fred. He** *came from Yorkshire.*
She married **my uncle Fred, who** *came from Yorkshire.*

She was engaged to **my cousin Jack.** *She loved* **him** *dearly.*
She was engaged to **my cousin Jack, whom** *she loved dearly.*

This is **the town hall. It** *was built in the last century.*
This is **the town hall, which** *was built in the last century.*

Joseph Conrad came to live in **England.** *He considered* **it** *his adopted country.*
Joseph Conrad came to live in **England, which** *he considered his adopted country.*

This is **Sally. Her** *horse won the Derby last week.*
This is **Sally, whose** *horse won the Derby last week.*

This is **Sally.** *You met* **her** *parents at the dinner last night.*
This is **Sally, whose** *parents you met at the dinner last night.*

■ Join these pairs of sentences, using a non-defining relative clause.
  1 Jack works in Christie's Cement Factory. It belongs to his father-in-law.

2 He married Jane Christie. She used to live next door to us.
3 It came as quite a shock to Jack to meet old Mr Christie. He had never spoken to him before.
4 To encourage the young people, Mr Christie gave them the house opposite. He had built it himself.
5 On the whole this was an advantage to Jack. His parents were opposed to the wedding.
6 The young couple get on quite well with Mr Christie. They borrow his money whenever it suits them.

B Contact clauses

Notice how the relative pronoun is omitted in the second sentence in each case:

The man whom/that you saw was Chinese.
The man you saw was Chinese.

The book that/which I wanted to borrow was expensive.
The book I wanted to borrow was expensive.

Contact clauses can be used for defining relative clauses in the object form.
The relative pronoun is omitted.
They cannot be used for defining relative clauses employing the possessive form *whose*.
The relative pronoun is not omitted in a non-defining relative clause.

■ Complete the following sentences with the correct relative pronoun where necessary.
1 The girl _____ you were speaking to is my cousin Mary.
My cousin Mary, _____ you were speaking to just now, has a great admiration for your work.
2 This house, _____ was built over a hundred years ago, is still occupied by the same family.
The house _____ my grandfather built over a hundred years ago is still standing.
3 His faithful comrade, Frank Martin, with _____ he had been associated all his life, eventually succeeded him as leader of the party.
His faithful comrade, Frank Martin, the man _____ he had been most closely associated with all his life, eventually succeeded him as leader of the party.
4 Sally is the girl _____ horse I was telling you about.
Sally, _____ horse won the race last Saturday, is thinking of entering it for the Derby.

C Where, when, why

Compare these pairs of sentences:

Do you know (the street) where he lives?
Descartes Street, where I live, was named after the philosopher.

Was that (the day) when it rained all morning?
The year 1914, when the First World War broke out, marked the end of nineteenth-century values.

Have you any idea of (the reason) why these things happen?
She resigned because of her bad health, which made it impossible for her to do her job properly.

Relative adverbs are found in defining and non-defining clauses. In non-defining clauses they are used with specific places, times or reasons and a comma always separates the relative pronoun from the place, time, etc.

■ Complete the following sentences with appropriate relative pronouns, and add the commas where necessary.
1 His daughter applied to enter the university _____ he had studied years ago.
His daughter applied to enter the University of Cambridge, _____ he had studied himself.
2 At the time _____ I met her, she was an artist.
At that time _____ I first met her, she was an artist.
3 I expect employees to give me a reason _____ they are late.
I was late because of the bus strike _____ made it necessary for me to come by underground.
4 The town _____ I grew up has changed in recent years.
Farley _____ I grew up has changed in recent years.
5 In 1957 _____ my brother was born I was still living there.
I was still living there _____ my brother was born.

D Use of the comma

Notice how the comma is used in non-defining relative clauses:

John Smith, who built this house, was my uncle.
The Mediterranean Sea, which is almost a lake, has been called the cradle of Western civilisation.

Non-defining relative clauses are always preceded by a comma, whether they appear in parenthesis in the middle of the sentence or at the end. It is useful to remember that any proper name will require a comma in a relative clause, since it defines itself.

There are rare exceptions to this rule, e.g., when there is more than one John Smith:

I don't know **the John Smith you are talking about.**

■ Punctuate the following letter to a magazine with commas only where they are necessary.

> Dear Sir,
> My father who works in an office in London says the country is going to the dogs. I think he means that there are too many places like the greyhound stadium that is near our house where my Uncle Bert goes every Wednesday. My mother who is a teacher says 'going to the dogs' is just an expression which means that it is a phrase people use when they cannot think of the precise words. She says my father means there are too many people in the country like my Uncle Bert who doesn't go to work. My sister Jenny who reads your column every day says you are the sort of person that can solve my probem because she has read letters from people whose questions you answered. Do you think my father means there are too many people who go to greyhound races or there are too many people who don't work? My Uncle Bert fits into both categories.
> (Paul Murray, aged 10)

■ Complete the following passage, using the correct relative adverb where necessary. Also put in commas where necessary. You will probably find it easier to put in the commas first.

Bath owes its name to the fact that it grew up around the Roman baths _____ (1) were among the largest in the Roman Empire. The city _____ (2) now has a population of over 80,000 people still has centres _____ (3) treat people with rheumatic diseases with the mineral waters _____ (4) first attracted the Romans to the spot.
The main attraction of Bath today, however, is its architecture much of _____ (5) dates from the eighteenth century _____ (6) it became a fashionable centre for aristocratic visitors _____ (7) overeating and drinking caused them to suffer from gout. John Wood the Elder designed the Circus _____ (8) was begun in 1754 and John Wood the Younger was responsible for Royal Crescent _____ (9) faces a sloping lawn _____ (10) runs down towards a park. The Pump Room _____ (11) is mentioned in the novels of Jane Austen _____ (12) lived in Bath at the beginning of the nineteenth century is also worth a visit.

At the time _____ (13) Jane Austen lived there the Assembly Rooms _____ (14) now house one of the finest costume museums in the world were the place _____ (15) people met for dances, as their name suggests. The feature _____ (16) makes them particularly attractive today is that sections of streets have been recreated with life-size figures all of _____ (17) are dressed in the costume of the period.
The main sporting attraction of Bath is its rugby team _____ (18) is among the best in the country but there are also two golf courses nearby both of _____ (19) are open to the public and there are plenty of courts in the parks _____ (20) visitors can play tennis. Those _____ (21) are interested in football should go to Bristol _____ (22) is only a short drive away _____ (23) there are two professional teams.
Bath is one of the most beautiful places _____ (24) I have visited in England and is certainly a city _____ (25) visitors from abroad are always welcome.

[1]4
Coordinate relative clauses

Compare these sentences:

We decided to meet outside **the Town Hall, which** *seemed the most convenient place.*
It started raining while Sarah was waiting for me outside the Town Hall, which *put her in a bad mood.*

The first sentence contains a non-defining relative clause (see Exercise 3); **which** refers to the Town Hall. It seemed the most convenient place to meet. The second sentence contains a coordinate relative clause; **which** here refers to the whole of the previous clause. The fact that it started raining while Sarah was waiting put her in a bad mood, not the Town Hall.
Which is the only relative pronoun found with coordinate relative clauses, whereas non-defining clauses could have **who**, **whom**, **which**, etc.

■ Decide whether the following sentences contain non-defining relative or coordinate relative clauses.

1 a) In the eighteenth century many people went to Bath, which had become a fashionable resort for the rich.
    b) In the eighteenth century many people went to Bath, which enabled them to enjoy themselves and cure their gout at the same time.

2 a) Visitors can hire clubs at the golf course, which saves them the trouble of travelling with them.
   b) Visitors can hire clubs at the golf course, which is quite near the city.
3 a) Jane Austen mentions Bath in *Northanger Abbey*, which is perhaps her most amusing novel.
   b) Jane Austen mentions Bath in *Northanger Abbey*, which shows how she employed her personal knowledge of places in her work.
4 a) A friend of mine supports Bristol City, which is one of the two football teams in the city.
   b) He never has a good word to say for Bristol Rovers, which suggests he may be rather biassed!
5 a) Some friends of ours sent us a postcard of Pulteney Bridge, which is one of the most interesting sights in Bath.
   b) Some friends of ours sent us a postcard of Pulteney Bridge, which was kind of them.

[2] 5

Revision of tenses: Present Simple and Present Continuous

Compare these sentences:

I get up early and study for an hour before breakfast.

(Regular action, personal habit.)

I am working hard at the moment. I am writing a book.

(Continuous action in present time, but not always at this moment, precisely. At this moment, the speaker may be explaining his problems to a friend.)

Sometimes I feel tired, but I like writing.

Verbs not usually used in continuous forms

Certain verbs are almost never found in continuous forms. They are mainly verbs connected with senses, mental processes, wishes, appearance and possession. Here is a list of the most common ones:

hear, notice, recognise, see, smell*, taste
believe, feel (that), think (that)*
know, mean, suppose, understand
forget, remember*
care, dislike, hate, love, want, wish
appear (= seem), **seem**
belong to, consist of, contain, have (= own, possess)
matter
refuse

* Note the following:
That smells good. (intransitive)
She is smelling the rose. (transitive)
What do you think? (What is your opinion?)
What are you thinking? (What thoughts are going through your mind?)
Do you remember our schooldays? (Have you any memory of them?)
Are you remembering our schooldays? (Are memories going through your mind?)

Note that these tenses are also used in future time:

If/When I see her, I will tell her that you asked after her.
We are having a party on Saturday. (already planned)
His plane arrives at 11.00 tomorrow morning. (fixed timetable)

■ Complete the paragraph below, using appropriate verbs and putting them in the correct tense, Present Simple or Present Continuous

We _____ (1) in the country and have several children so we always _____ (2) early. My husband is a pop-singer. If he (not) _____ (3), he (always) _____ (4) down to breakfast at the same time. Some people _____ (5) it is strange that we _____ (6) to live in the country, but my husband _____ (7) it a relaxation from the constant travelling when he _____ (8). When he _____ (9) abroad, we usually _____ (10) with him and _____ (11) a house for the children. Perhaps it _____ (12) wrong to take them everywhere but I _____ (13) how lonely I was when my parents were away and I _____ (14) my husband (not) _____ (15) being separated from the children because they are always his first thought, even when he _____ (16) in front of thousands of people. My husband _____ (17) me to join him in the group, but whenever he _____ (18) me, I always _____ (19). The excitement of being a pop-star (not) _____ (20) very much to me, but when I _____ (21) in the country and I _____ (22) the wind blowing through my hair, I am happy. (not)(you) _____ (23) I have made the right decision? Or (you) _____ (24): 'This woman (just) _____ (25) a good public relations job for her husband'?

[2] 6

Revision of tenses: Past Simple and Past Continuous

The Past Simple and Past Continuous tenses are found in three basic combinations:

*When the telephone **rang**, he **answered** it.* (One action after another.)

*When the telephone **rang**, he **was having** a bath.* (Continuous action before, and possibly after, the single action.)

*While he **was having** a bath, his wife **was cooking** the dinner.* (Two actions continuing at the same time in the past.)

Note that we do not use the Past Continuous tense for habitual action in the past. We use **used to**, in contrast to the present, or the Past Simple for historical events without contrast, irrespective of the length of time.

*He **used to be** a pop singer, but now he just **lies** on the beach in California.*
*Shakespeare **was born** in Stratford-on-Avon, and **died** there, but he **spent** much of his life in London.*

Change the paragraph in Exercise 5 from present to past time. Imagine that the narrator is an old lady, now a widow, remembering her youth. There is no need to use *used to*.

[2] 7

Revision of tenses: Past Simple and Past Perfect Simple and Continuous

The Past Perfect tense is used to refer to time previous to the main action when the main action is in the Past Simple.

*He **had** already **written** several books **before** he **became** well-known.*
*He **didn't realise** how much the cost of living **had gone up** while he **had been living** abroad.*
***By the time** I got to the station, the train **had left**.*
*I **had been working** so hard in the garden all morning that I **was** quite hungry **by the time** lunch **was** ready.*

■ Complete the paragraph below, using appropriate verbs and putting them in the correct tense, Past Simple, Past Perfect Simple or Past Perfect Continuous. Note the position of adverbs.

I usually visit my customers by car, but yesterday I had to go to Croydon by train because my car is being serviced. At the station in London, I bought a crime novel and found it so interesting that when I _____(1) up I (already) _____(2) the third chapter. At the same time I suddenly _____(3) that the train (just)_____(4) Croydon and was on its way to Brighton. I _____(5) so interested in the book that I (not)_____(6) the train stopping. By the time I eventually _____(7) the customer, I _____(8) backwards and forwards on the railway for over two hours, but I could hardly tell him that I was so late because I _____(9) a book and (not)_____(10) out at the right station. I _____(11) I _____(12) an accident in the car, which was true, apart from the fact that the accident _____(13) three days earlier.

[2] 8

It's + adjective + *for/that*

Compare these sentences:

*It's **fashionable** for some intellectuals to sympathise with poor people without doing anything to help them.*
*It's **obvious** that they are not really sympathetic if they do nothing to help.*

In some cases, the adjective may be followed by either construction but usually we prefer one or the other. Among the adjectives followed by **for** are: **boring, dangerous, difficult, easy, expensive, healthy, necessary**.
Among those followed by **that** are: **certain, clear, curious, likely, lucky, probably, surprising, true**.
Note the use of **interesting** with the two constructions:

*It would be **interesting** for you to study abroad.* (You would find it interesting.)
*It's **interesting** that he made you that offer.* (I find it interesting.)

■ Use the adjectives and verbs given in brackets in constructions like those above to complete these sentences.

1 (clear) that he didn't work very hard.
2 (difficult) me (understand) why he took that job.
3 (dangerous) them (work) in such conditions.
4 (likely) that the factory will be closed soon.
5 (expensive) him (travel) to work by train.
6 (lucky) you didn't take the job they offered you.
7 (easy) them (criticise). They're not responsible for the project. But (curious) they didn't say anything at the outset.
8 (true) we haven't had a very successful year so far, although (not necessary) us to worry about it.

[2] 9

As and *like*

As refers to a person's profession or a part he plays as an actor; *like* is only used for comparison.

> *He works **as** an engineer. (He is an engineer.)*
> *She was wonderful **as** Cleopatra. (. . . in the part of Cleopatra.)*
> *He climbs **like** a monkey. (Comparison: He is not a monkey.)*

■ Complete these sentences with **as** or **like**.

1 He could swim _____ a fish.
2 He works _____ a fisherman.
3 I once appeared on the stage _____ Othello, but I'm glad I'm not _____ him in real life.
4 He has taken his responsibilities _____ Managing Director so much to heart that he goes around behaving _____ Napoleon.
5 I once had a friend who was in his father's class at school. He never knew whether his father was speaking to him _____ a father or _____ a teacher.

[3] 10

Revision of tenses: Present Perfect Simple and Continuous and Past Simple

Study the examples to remind yourself of the combinations of tenses used before attempting the exercise.

> *He **has written** several novels. Most of them **have been** quite successful, but the last one **didn't get** very good reviews.*
> *I've **been** to Paris twice. The first time I **went** by boat and train, but when I **made** the journey last year, I **flew**.*
> *He **has** only **come** to class once this week. He **was** here on Monday, but we **haven't seen** him since then.*

> He's **been** an artist
> He's **been painting** { for twenty years.
> since he was a boy.
> all his life. }

> He **began** painting { twenty years ago.
> when he was very young. }

> *He **taught** art at the Academy for twenty years (but now he's retired).*
> *He's **been teaching** art at the Academy for twenty years and he still enjoys the classes. (The Present Perfect Simple could be used here.)*

*When you've **been** to a lot of interviews for jobs and **been turned down** every time, you **lose confidence** in yourself. When he **was turned down** at the interview, he **lost confidence** in himself.*

■ Complete the paragraph below, using appropriate verbs and putting them in the correct tense, Present Perfect Simple, Present Perfect Continuous or Past Simple. Be careful with the position of the adverb.

I suppose one's view of the countryside is coloured by one's past experience. For example, I (always) _____ (1) of Yorkshire as cold and inhospitable although the people I _____ (2) who _____ (3) from there have always been warm and friendly. It is probably because I _____ (4) two years there in the army, doing National Service. Of course, that _____ (5) twenty years ago, but I don't imagine the climate _____ (6) much since then. I (never) _____ (7) that first winter in Yorkshire. It _____ (8) very cold and the snow _____ (9) every day for two months. One morning, about four o'clock, I _____ (10) on guard when a man _____ (11) at the camp on a motor-cycle. He had come to light the boilers. He said he _____ (12) it every morning. He (not) _____ (13) to mind the weather. 'I _____ (14) up early all my life, son,' he _____ (15). 'I _____ (16) this bike through snow and ice for twenty years. If you (never)_____ (17) in the north, you don't know what bad weather's like.' I (always)_____ (18) an admiration for that man, and the last time I was on guard I _____ (19) goodbye to him, but I (never)_____ (20) any desire to go back to that part of England since.

[3] 11

Word order: adverbs of frequency

Notice the position of the adverbs in these sentences:

A *Are you **always** here on Wednesdays?*
B *No, I'm **sometimes** at my mother's.*

A *Do you **always** play football on Wednesdays?*
B *No, I **sometimes** play tennis. I don't **always** play football. I can't **always** spare the time.*

A *Have you **ever** played squash?*
B *I've **only** played it once or twice. I've **never** taken it seriously. I've **often** been invited to play.*

*I would **never** have taken up golf if I couldn't have afforded it. But I have **always** been interested in it. If I hadn't practised regularly, though, I would **never** have been chosen to play for the club.*

The normal position of these adverbs is *before* the main verb and *after* the auxiliary (or after the first one if there is more than one). In the present tense of 'to be' they come *after* the main verb.

■ Complete the sentences below, putting the adverbs in brackets in the correct position in the phrase or sentence they follow.

1   When I worked in London, the trains were not late (always). They arrived on time (occasionally). What I can forget (never) is the voice that greeted us (always) when we arrived at Victoria. I think it was a record that was put on (always) in the mornings of a woman who sounded bored (always): 'We are sorry your train is late. This is due to circumstances beyond our control.' They may have changed the record (sometimes) as the excuses were different (occasionally), and it has occurred to me (sometimes) that the woman's voice may have been (actually) real.
2   If I had not seen it with my own eyes (just) I would have believed it (never).
3   He would have been convinced (never), although he has been told about it (frequently), if you had not taken him to see it for himself.
4   How could you have imagined it (ever)?
5   He must have wondered (often) if he would have been given the job (ever) if the boss had not been an old friend of the family.

[3] 12

Like and *such as*

Compare these sentences:

A lot of famous people have visited his restaurant – for example/for instance, Sophia Loren, Bob Dylan and Prince Charles.
Famous people, like/such as Sophia Loren, Bob Dylan and Prince Charles, have visited his restaurant.
Such famous people as Sophia Loren, Bob Dylan and Prince Charles have visited his restaurant.

Like and **such as** or **such . . . as** can be used as alternatives to **for example** or **for instance**. Notice that the phrase with **like** or **such as** follows the noun that it refers to as closely as possible.

■ Rewrite the following sentences, using **like/such as** and **such . . . as**. Make two new sentences in each case.

1   A number of famous country houses were built in the eighteenth century – for example, Chatsworth, Blenheim Palace and Castle Howard.
2   Castle Howard was used for the television series, 'Brideshead Revisited', in which a number of famous actors took part – for example, Jeremy Irons, Sir Laurence Olivier and John Gielgud.
3   The last two stars also appeared in a series about Wagner with other well-known actors – for example, Richard Burton, Vanessa Redgrave and Ralph Richardson.
4   A lot of great composers led interesting lives – for example, Mozart, Beethoven and Chopin.

[3] 13

As following certain verbs

Compare these sentences:

*He was **known as** the 'King of the Underworld'.* (It was his nickname, not his real name.)
*He was **known to be** the king of the underworld.* (He was in fact the head of criminal society.)
*He **treats** his students **as** friends.* (They are his friends.)
*He **treats** his students **like** animals.* (They are not animals.)

Common verbs of this type include: **accept, characterise, class, count, define, describe, express, interpret, know** (usually **be known**), **look on, recognise, regard, see, think of, treat, use.**

■ Rewrite the sentences below, using the verbs given in brackets and the **as** construction. Make whatever changes are necessary and leave out unnecessary words.

1   Someone once said that fox hunting was the unspeakable in pursuit of the uneatable. (define)
2   King Edward VII was commonly called 'the Peacemaker'. (know)
3   I consider his last book to be the best of his novels. (regard)
4   The blurb says it is tragic but I would put it into the category of black comedy. (describe) (class)
5   He behaves towards his staff as if they were equals, which is an improvement on his predecessor, who treated them like slaves. (treat) Of course, his predecessor never admitted anyone to be his equal. (accept)

[4] 14

Can, may, could, might

A can, could

Compare these sentences:

*I **can** run faster than you.*
*I **can** speak French.*
*I **could** run faster than my brother when we were young.*
*I **could** speak French when I was ten years old.*

Can/could express ability or capacity, including the idea of 'know how to'.

- Change these sentences into the Past form, using the time references provided in brackets.

  1 I can ride a bicycle. (eight years old)
  2 Can you swim? (a child)
  3 He can speak several languages. (at the age of ten)
  4 He can run 100m in 10 seconds. (at his peak)
  5 Can you beat your father at tennis? (at school)

B will be able to, have/has been able to

Compare these sentences with those in Section A:

*When I've had a few more lessons, **I'll be able to** speak French fluently.*
***Have you been able to** get in touch with him?*

The Future and Present Perfect forms of **can** are formed with **be able to**. However, in sentences relating to the near future, **can** is often used when there is no subordinate clause:

A Can you come tomorrow?
*B I'm not sure if I **can/will be able to**.*

- Transform the sentences from Section A into the Future and use them to complete these sentences:

  . . . when I finish this speed-reading course.
  ***I'll be able to read fast** when I finish this speed-reading course.*

  1 . . . when I've had a little more practice.
  2 . . . in time for our next summer holiday?
  3 . . . if he finishes his interpreters' course.
  4 . . . when he's been training for a few more months.
  5 . . . when you've improved your service?

- Look at this example and then use the information given to do the following exercise:

  A Have you ever read 'War and Peace'? (get beyond the first 200 pages)

B No. I've never been able to get beyond the first 200 pages.

  6 Have you ever been to Hawaii? (afford it)
  7 Have you ever eaten snails? (face the idea)
  8 Have you ever tried to make your own clothes? (find the time)
  9 Have you ever taken an interest in modern art? (understand it)
  10 Have you ever sung in a choir? (sing in tune)

C was able to and alternative forms

Compare these sentences:

*He **could** reach the books on the top shelf because he was tall.*
*He wasn't tall enough to reach the books on the top shelf, but when he got a ladder, he **was able to** get the one he wanted.*

When something was achieved in a particular instance in the past through an effort, we must use **was able to**, not **could**. Alternatively, we can use two other verbs, **managed to** + infinitive and **succeeded in** + gerund:

When he got a ladder, he { ***was able to reach*** / ***managed to reach*** / ***succeeded in reaching*** } *the book he wanted.*

- Change these sentences to each of the other two forms given. Be careful of word order.

  1 After queuing for hours, I finally managed to get a ticket.
  2 After several days' negotiations, they were eventually able to persuade the workers to return to work.
  3 He was thrown overboard when the boat was a mile out to sea but he eventually succeeded in swimming to the shore.
  4 After a morning spent at the post office, we were finally able to find out what had happened to the parcels.
  5 He spent years in his laboratory working on the disease but he eventually managed to find a cure.

D can, may, might (deduction)

Compare these sentences:

*We always think of Spain as hot and sunny but it **can** rain heavily there at times.*
*It **may/might** rain this afternoon.*

Can refers to a possibility that is always present, while **may** refers to a possibility in a particular case, and **might** to this possibility existing but being less likely.

- Complete the following dialogues with **can, may** or **might**.

1 A I'm sure I'm right.
   B You _____ (1) be right. I'm in no
      position to say. But everyone _____ (2)
      make mistakes. Why don't you show the
      results to someone else? They _____ (3)
      be able to confirm your opinion.
   B The trouble is that I don't know anyone
      sufficiently qualified to tell me. I suppose I
      _____ (4) find someone if I rang the
      Central Laboratories, but it's unlikely. No
      one has done this sort of work there before.
2 A What's the weather like? Is it going to be
      sunny this afternoon?
   B I'm not sure. It _____ (1) be, but we
      _____ (2) get a storm. I admit that it
      doesn't look like it at the moment, but the
      trouble is that storms _____ (3) spring
      up so quickly round here that you never
      know when to expect them. But we
      _____ (4) be lucky. There's no sign of
      trouble at the moment. It _____ (5) be
      wise not to go sailing, though. It'll probably
      be all right, but you shouldn't take any risks.

Note 1 Since **can** is directly related to **be able to**
         (see Sections B and C above) we cannot say
         'can be able to'.
      2 **It may not/might not be true** means
         'perhaps it isn't true' or 'it is possibly true'.
         It can't be true means 'there is no
         possibility of its being true'.

**E   can't have, could have, may have, might have
(deduction)**

Compare these responses to *A*'s question:

   A Why hasn't she arrived?
   *B She **can't have** got lost, can she?* (It's impossible,
      isn't it?)
      *She **may have** got lost.* (Perhaps she (has) got lost.)
      *She **might have** got lost.* (But it seems unlikely if
      she had a map.)
      *She **could have** got lost.* (Perhaps she got lost.)

The Past forms of **may, might, can** and **could**,
referring to possibility, are formed with **have** and the
past participle of the main verb. Since **can** (affirmative)
is only used for something that is always possible, it can
only appear in the Past in the negative form (**can't
have**).

■ In this exercise, think of as many explanations as you
  can for what **may have** happened. If they are
  unlikely, use **might have**. If they are impossible, use
  can't have.

Harry is a businessman, but he usually comes home
on time, unless he has a lot of work to do or he has
visitors. If he goes out in the evening with customers
he usually phones his wife but she was out from 4.00
till 6.00 at a friend's house. She didn't tell him she
was going to have tea with her friend.

Harry has not arrived home for dinner as usual at 7
o'clock. His wife is worried about him. She thinks of
various reasons why he is late. What possibilities
does she consider?

   e.g. **Harry may have had a lot of work to do.**

[5] 15

Had better, should/ought to

Compare these sentences:

   *I feel tired. I'**d better** go to bed.*
   *You don't look very well. You'**d better** go and see the doctor.*
   *You always look tired these days. You **should** go to bed
   earlier.*
   *You don't look very well. You **ought to** see a doctor* (but
   I don't suppose you will).

Had better means 'I think I (you, he, etc.) should' or
'It would be sensible (right) if I (you, he, etc.) . . .'
Had better is always followed by the infinitive without
to. The negative form **had better not** is used in the
same way:

   *He looks angry. I'**d better not** interrupt him.*
   *He'd be annoyed if he saw you doing that. You'**d better not**
   do it again.*

Should is preferable to **had better** when we are
speaking in general terms. The negative form
shouldn't is used in the same way:

   *You **shouldn't** interrupt him when he's working. It always
   makes him angry.*

Note that you'**d better not interrupt him** means that
you haven't interrupted him yet, but you **shouldn't
interrupt him** means that you already have, or
frequently do so.
Ought to is the same as **should**, and **ought not to** the
same as **shouldn't**. However, compared with **had
better**, it suggests that the sensible idea will not be
carried out:

   *You **ought to** take more exercise* (but I don't expect you
   will).

■ Complete the following sentences with a form of **had
  better** or **should/ought to**, choosing whichever
  seems most appropriate to the context.

19

1 I've lost my passport.
   You _____ go to the consulate and report it.
2 I've cut myself shaving again.
   You _____ be more careful.
3 I've never been to Paris before so I _____ buy a map of the Metro.
4 He's always getting lost when he goes out in the car. He _____ buy a map. I've told him so hundreds of times.
5 You _____ (negative) say anything about the boss. He's over there and he might hear you.
6 You _____ (negative) criticise the boss in front of other people. It gives them a bad impression of the firm.
7 I know I _____ (negative) argue with him because it raises his blood pressure, but somehow I can't help it.
8 I _____ (negative) argue with him. He looks dangerous.

[5] 16

Purpose clauses

A Purpose: *for, to, because*; cause: *because*

Compare these sentences:

A **What**'s that brush **for**?
B It's **for cleaning** typewriters (with).
A **What** do you want that brush **for**?
B **To clean** my typewriter (with).
A **Why** do you want that brush?
B **Because I want to clean** my typewriter (with it).
A **Why** are you cleaning your typewriter?
B **Because** it's dirty.

We use **for** with the gerund to talk about the function of a thing; we use the infinitive to talk about the purpose of an action.
Why? questions can refer to purpose, as in the third example (answered by the infinitive or a clause with **because**), or cause, as in the fourth example (answered by a clause with **because**).

■ Give suitable answers to the following questions.

   1 June has a badminton racquet. Her little brother asks:
      a What's that racquet for?
      b What do you want that racquet for?
      c Why are you putting that racquet in your bag? (Use **going to**.)

2 Harry has a special camera. He takes pictures with it underwater. A friend asks:
   a What's that camera for?
   b What do you want that camera for?
   c Why are you unpacking that camera? (Use **going to**.)
3 Rose has a special calculator. It does statistical calculations. Her husband asks:
   a What's that calculator for?
   b What do you want that calculator for?
   c Why are you bringing that calculator with you? (Use **going to**.)

B *to, in order (not) to, so as (not) to*

Compare these sentences:

We took the children to the cinema
{
to keep them happy.
in order to keep them happy.
so as to keep them happy.
in order not to disappoint them.
so as not to disappoint them.
}

Note that the order of the clauses could be reversed in all cases, but this is most common with **in order to** and **so as to**, which usually appear in more formal contexts:

In order to avoid disturbance of the peace, the Government has decreed that no public meetings will be held in the square until further notice.

The infinitive without **in order** or **so as** cannot be used in the negative.

■ Rewrite each of the phrases in italics in these sentences, using one of the phrases given above.

   1 He came in quietly *because he didn't want to* wake his wife.
   2 They bought some champagne *because they wanted to* celebrate the end of the course.
   3 *Since they wanted to* explain the situation to the public, the Government put a special programme on television.
   4 He booked a ticket for the performance *because he wanted to* make sure of getting in.
   5 He booked a ticket for the performance *because he didn't want to* have to stand in a queue.
   6 *As he didn't want to* stand in a queue, he booked a ticket for the performance.
   7 *If you wish to* make sure of a seat at the performance, you are advised to book in advance.
   8 *To avoid boring* you, I'll make this the last sentence in the exercise.

C *So that* with change of subject

Compare these sentences:

> *He spoke slowly **to help** them understand him.*
> *He spoke slowly **so that they would** understand him.*

When the subject is understood from the main clause, we usually use the infinitive; if the subject changes, we use **so that** or **in order that**. Exceptions are verbs taking two objects (**give**, **send**, etc.):

> *I gave her a ring **to wear** on her finger.* (She wore it.)
> *I sent him to the baker's **to buy** some bread.* (He bought it.)

However, this is only true if there is no doubt about who did the action.

■ Join the following sentences together with **to** to make single sentences, using **so that/in order that** only where it is necessary for the meaning.

1 He sent them to university. He wanted to give them a good education.
2 He sent them to university. He wanted them to have a good education.
3 He sent them to the university. He told them to put their names down for the entrance examination.
4 I've left her a note. I want to tell her where to meet us.
5 I've left her a note. I want her to know where to meet us.
6 He's sold his house. He wants to pay his brother's debts.
7 He's sold his house. He wants his brother to be able to pay his debts.
8 He's given his brother some money. Then his brother can pay his debts.
9 He's employed a nurse. He wants his mother to be looked after.
10 He's employed a nurse. He wants her to look after his mother.

[5] 17

Must have . . . and had to . . .

Compare these sentences:

> *I couldn't understand him at first because he had such a strong Yorkshire accent. **I had to** ask him to repeat the question.*
> *He had a strong Yorkshire accent although he came from London. He **must have** lived in Yorkshire for a long time.*

Had to is used as the Past tense form of **must** and **have to** to imply that an obligation existed; **must have** is the Past form of **must** implying that we were almost certain that something was true, because this was a logical conclusion.

■ Complete the paragraph below, using appropriate verbs either in the form **had to** + infinitive or in the form **must have** + past participle, according to the sense of the context.

When I did my military service, I _____(1) with the same fear of sergeants as everyone else, but by the time I finished I _____(2) that they were not such inhuman people as I had imagined. It is true that at the start we _____(3) all sorts of unpleasant things and the sergeants _____(4) themselves, because they always shouted at us and laughed among themselves. Some of those men _____(5) sadists. One day, however, I _____(6) a telegraph pole and almost killed myself. I _____(7) quickly or I would have fallen from a great height. The sergeant who was watching _____(8) his mind about me because afterwards he always treated me kindly. Later on, I went abroad, and there everything was different. We _____(9) a lot of work and we knew we _____(10) together. The sergeant in charge of my section was called Fish, which _____(11) a lot of people laugh but we were so fond of him that we would never have done so. Looking back, I suppose we _____(12) him as a kind of father.

[5] 18

Personal and impersonal constructions with *seem, appear*, etc.

Compare these sentences:

> *It seems that they're out.*
> *They're out, it seems.*
> *They seem to be out.*

> *It appears that they haven't heard us ringing.*
> *They haven't heard us ringing, it appears.*
> *They don't appear to have heard us ringing.*

> *It turned out that they didn't know we were coming.*
> *They didn't know we were coming, it turned out.*
> *They turned out not to have known we were coming.*

■ Change the construction of each of the following sentences from the one given to each of the other two.

1 It seems that the Headmaster is angry.
2 It appears that you're a stranger here.
3 They've been waiting a long time, it seems.

4 They hadn't made any preparations for our visit, it turned out.

5 It seems that he doesn't care whether he upsets people or not.

6 You don't appear to know who I am.

7 They haven't played this game before, it appears.

8 It turned out that they hadn't been told we were coming.

[5] 19

Reflexive verbs

A number of common verbs in English are often found in reflexive constructions:

1 Action, pain, danger: **burn, cut, defend, hurt, kill, drown, shoot.**

> She **burned herself** on the hot iron.

2 Behaviour, emotion: **amuse, behave, blame, control, deceive, enjoy, be ashamed of, be sorry for, feel sorry for**.

> He was an only child, so he had to learn to **amuse himself**.

3 Thought, speech: **consider, count, express, say to, talk to, tell, think**. **Count** and **think** are included with the meaning of 'consider'.

> **Consider (count, think) yourself** lucky that you escaped.

4 Action not normally reflexive: **congratulate, educate, fling, introduce, invite, teach, throw**.

> He's trying to **teach himself** Russian.

5 Others: **can't help, prevent, stop, weigh.**

> I wish I could **stop myself** smoking.

■ Use one of the following verbs in the correct form once only to complete these sentences, together with a suitable reflexive pronoun (**myself, yourself, themselves**, etc.).

be ashamed of, blame, consider, drown, enjoy, feel sorry for, introduce, kill, shoot, weigh

1 I _____ very much at the party. I had a wonderful time.

2 You should _____. I've never seen such shocking behaviour.

3 I don't think we've met before. Allow me to _____.

4 When his team lost in the last minute of the game, the goalkeeper sat in the goal _____.

5 She's on a diet, so she _____ every morning.

6 It was one of those Russian plays where you know the hero is going to _____, but you're not sure whether he will _____ in the river, _____ with a pistol, or cut his wrists and bleed to death.

7 Don't _____ for what happened. It wasn't your fault.

8 Under the circumstances, I think that we can _____ fortunate that nothing worse happened.

[6] 20

Must, should, ought to, and past forms

Compare these sentences:

> I **must** take my medicine three times a day. Otherwise, I'd be very ill.
> He **has to** take his medicine three times a day. The doctor told him to.

> He $\begin{Bmatrix} \textbf{\textit{should}} \\ \textbf{\textit{ought to}} \end{Bmatrix}$ take his medicine three times a day, but he often forgets.

> I **had to take** my medicine three times a day when I was ill.

> He $\begin{Bmatrix} \textbf{\textit{should have}} \\ \textbf{\textit{ought to have}} \end{Bmatrix}$ **taken** his medicine before breakfast, but he forgot.

Must suggests a sense of personal responsibility, **have to** that responsibility has been imposed from outside, **should** and **ought to** that the responsibility exists but may not be carried out.

Had to is the past of **have to**; **should have** and **ought to have**, are the past forms of **should** and **ought to**. (See also Exercise 17 for **must have**.)

■ Complete the sentences below, using **had to** + infinitive or **should have/ought to have** + past participle of the verb given in brackets.

1 (get up)
a) I _____ early when I was in the army, and the sergeant came round to make sure we did.
b) I _____ early this morning, because I had an appointment at 9 o'clock, but I forgot to set the alarm.

2 (renew)
a) I _____ my passport last week. Otherwise, it would have been out of date.

b) You _____ your passport before now. As it is, I cannot allow you to leave the country.

3 (get)

a) He felt that he _____ the job, but the interviewer was prejudiced against him.

b) He _____ the job because he could not see any other way of feeding his family.

4 (drive)

a) I _____ carefully because the road was icy.

b) You _____ more carefully on such an icy road.

5 (sell)

a) I _____ my house last year, because I needed the money.

b)

I _____ mine, too. If I had, I would have got a better price for it than I could now.

[7] 21

Reported speech – tense, time and place changes

Compare these sentences:

He said, 'I don't like onions'. (direct)
*He said **he didn't like onions**.* (reported)
She said, 'I visited my aunt yesterday'. (direct)
*She said **that she had visited her aunt the day before**.* (reported)

Notice that when we change direct speech to reported speech, expressions of time and place (e.g. **yesterday**) often change. The tense will change also if the verb introducing the reported speech is in the Past tense (e.g. **said**). Use these lists of rules for reference in answering the questions in the exercise below.

A Basic tense changes

DIRECT	REPORTED
'I'm working very hard.'	He said **he was working** . . .
'I earn £100 a week.'	He said he **earned** . . .
'I'm going to change my job.'	He said **he was going** to . . .
'I'll finish it soon.'	He said **he would finish** it . . .
'I've never seen her before.'	He said **he had** never **seen** her . . .
'I didn't break it.'	He said **he hadn't broken** it.
'I can run faster than Mary.'	He said **he could run** faster . . .
'It may be too late.'	He said **it might be** . . .
'I must go.'	He said **he had to** go.
'I'll have to go.'	He said **he would have to** go.

Note There is no change for **should** or **ought to**.

B Time and place changes

DIRECT	REPORTED
here	there
this	that (the)
these	those (the)
this (pron)	it
that (pron)	it
now	then, at that time
yesterday	the day before, the previous day
tomorrow	the day after, the following day
last week	the week before, the previous week
next week	the week after, the following week
ago	before

C More complex tense changes

As already indicated in reported speech, **may** is always changed to **might** and **can** to **could**. Might and **could** do not change, however, and **may** and **might**, **can** and **could** do not change to **may have**, **might have**, etc:

'I don't think it will rain, although it might.'
He said he didn't think it would rain, although it might.
'If I knew what the problem was, I could help her.'
He said that if he knew what the problem was, he could help her.

The only other changes required, therefore, are from **can't have** to **couldn't have** and from **may have/may not have** to **might have/might not have**:

'Anyone who thinks the newspaper article is insulting can't have read it properly.'
He said that anyone who thought the newspaper article was insulting couldn't have read it properly.
'There's no reason to get upset. John may have stopped at the pub for a drink.'
He told her there was no reason to get upset. John might have stopped at the pub for a drink.

In the same way, **should** does not change to **should have**:

> *'You should go and see the doctor.'*
> **He said I should go and see the doctor.**

Should have, of course, does not change, either:

> *'You should have taken your medicine after breakfast.'*
> **He said I should have taken my medicine after breakfast.**

Must, implying a logical conclusion, does not change in reported speech:

> *'They must be there.'*
> **He said that they must be there.**
> *'They must have been there, but now they've gone.'*
> **He said that they must have been there, but now they had gone.**

■ Change the sentences below from direct to reported speech. Where necessary, include appropriate pronoun forms, such as **me**, **him**, **her**, and be careful to make any necessary changes to time and place references.

1 'I haven't seen them since last year.' (She . . .)
2 'I'm not going to do that till next week.' (He . . .)
3 'I didn't expect to see you here.' (She . . .)
4 'I can't deal with this until tomorrow.' (He . . .)
5 'The Browns may know where it is.' (She . . .)
6 'I must go to the doctor's next week.' (He . . .)
7 'By the time we get there, the train will have left.' (They . . .)
8 'If you saw him last night at 10 o'clock, he can't have gone very far.' (She . . .)
9 'When you spoke to them yesterday, they may not have understood how important the problem is.' (He said . . .)
10 'You should have told me where I could find it. In that case, I would not have spent hours looking for it.' (She said . . .)

[8] 22

One, ones and possessive forms

A   *one, ones, it, some*

Compare these sentences:

> *Tape recorders are quite cheap in this country. You can buy* **one** *for a few pounds, though* **the best ones** *are usually exported. Why don't you buy* **one***?*

> *Cheese is quite cheap here. You can buy* **it** *at 50 pence for half a kilo, though* **the best of it** *is usually exported. Why don't you buy* **some***?*

We can use **one** or **ones** in place of a noun in the singular or plural that has already been mentioned, e.g., **tape recorders.**
But we cannot use **one** or **ones** with mass nouns, e.g., **cheese**.

■ Complete these sentences with the correct form, **one**, **ones**, **it** or **some**.

A   I'd like to buy _____(1) fruit. What's _____(2) like here?
B   Well, most of _____(3) is exported. But we can get _____(4) in this shop.
A   Melons are in season now. I bought a very good _____(5) yesterday. The big _____(6) are quite juicy.
B   That's a good idea. I'll get _____(7).

B   *this one, these red ones,* etc.

Compare the singular and plural in these sentences.

> A   *I'm looking for a radio.* **That (black) one** *looks all right.*
> B   *Do you mean* **this** *one?*
> A   *No,* **the one** *I mean is* **that big one** *in the window.*
> A   *I'd like some apples.* **Those** *look quite juicy.*
> B   *Do you mean* **these***?*
> A   *No,* **the ones** *I mean are* **those big red ones** *in the window.*

We can use **one** with **this**, **that**, **the** and adjectives, but in the plural we can only use **ones** with **these** and **those** if there is an adjective, too.

■ Complete these sentences with the correct form, **one**, **ones**, **this**, **that**, **these** or **those**.

A   I want a scarf for my wife. A silk _____(1) if you have one.
B   Certainly, sir. _____(2) in the tray here are all silk. How about _____(3) green _____(4)?
A   No, my wife doesn't like green. _____(5) red _____(6) would suit her better, perhaps, or one of _____(7) blue _____(8), I'm not sure.
B   There are some more in the window, sir. _____(9) red _____(10) hanging on its own may be what you're looking for, and there are _____(11) in the corner, too, though they're more expensive.

A Never mind. I'd like to see _____(12), and can you bring _____(13) pink _____(14), too? I think that may be the _____(15) that would suit my wife best.

C Possessive forms

Compare these sentences:

My situation is not the same as { ***his.***
the one *he is involved in.*

Our problems are not the same as { ***theirs.***
the ones *they have to face.*

Her novels are not as good as { ***Jane Austen's.***
the ones *Jane Austen wrote.*

We cannot use **one** or **ones** with possessive forms.

■ Complete these sentences with the correct form, **one**, **ones**, **ours** or **yours**.

A Let's take a taxi. Look, there's _____(1) over there. Taxis seem a lot cheaper here than the _____(2) in London.
B It depends. The _____(3) that come from the airport charge extra, but this _____(4) won't cost much. Of course the difference between our taxis and _____(5), I mean the _____(6) you have in London, is that _____(7) are normal cars, whereas _____(8) are specially designed. Personally, I can't understand how you can put up with those old-fashioned black _____(9).
A No, I don't know why, either. They don't hold any more people and they're not nearly so comfortable as _____(10).

[9] 23

Emphatic constructions: *it, what, the thing that*

A General statements

Compare these sentences:

I don't mind the noise in cities. { ***What bothers me is the smoke.***
The thing that bothers me is the smoke.
It's the smoke that bothers me.

What (first example) means the same as **the thing that** (second example), but notice the form of the third construction. This form, called a cleft sentence, can be used to emphasise almost any part of a sentence except the verb.

■ Rewrite the final sentence in each of the following in two ways, using the alternative constructions given above.

1 I don't mind flying. The thing that annoys me is the time you have to spend in airports.
2 Oh, really? What upsets me is the rudeness of the employees.
3 I have a different complaint from you two. It's the inefficiency of the services that gets me down.
4 Yes, you're right. The thing that I really can't stand is the so-called shuttle service, like the one from Barcelona to Madrid.
5 Oh, you've had trouble with that, too, have you? I arrived there last week at 8 o'clock and there were no planes with vacant seats till after 12.00, the man told me. But the thing that annoyed me most was the smile on his face.
6 Yes, I understand. It's not really their fault in Barcelona, though. It's the fact that nearly all the planes leave from Madrid that causes the trouble.

B Statements referring to place

Compare these sentences:

We didn't meet the Smiths in Rome. { ***We met them in Naples.***
The place where we met them was Naples.
It was in Naples that (where) we met them.

The second and third sentences are emphatic forms of the first.

■ Rewrite the second of each of the pairs of sentences below in two ways, using the emphatic forms.

1 The capital of the United States is Washington. But the real action takes place in New York.
2 Shakespeare was brought up in Stratford-on-Avon. But he made his name in London.
3 They don't really breed the best racehorses in England. They breed them in Ireland.
4 He wasn't really happy in the city. He was only truly content in his native village.
5 The Nile is not spectacular at its source. It becomes a great river at Khartoum.

C Statements referring to time

Compare these sentences:

The mosquitoes don't bother us in winter. { ***They are a nuisance in summer.***
It's in summer when (that) they are a nuisance.

■ Rewrite the second of each of the pairs of sentences below in the emphatic form.

1 Floods are not a major risk in spring. We have to be on the watch in autumn.
2 Tourists do not come in great numbers in July. Most of them come in August.
3 He did not write his best plays as a young man. He wrote them in middle age.
4 The French Revolution began in a disorganised manner. The decisive event, the storming of the Bastille, took place on 14th July, 1789.
5 The Americans did not obtain their freedom from Britain until 1783. But they celebrate Independence Day on July 4th, commemorating the Declaration of Independence of 1776.

[9] 24
As if/as though

Notice that the forms are interchangeable:

*It looks **as if/as though** it's **going** to rain.*
*It looked **as if/as though** it **was going** to rain.*

*You talk **as if/as though** it **rained** all the time in England.* (It doesn't.)
*He behaves **as if/as though** he **were/was** the king.* (He isn't.)
*He speaks **as if/as though** he **had won** the Nobel Prize.* (He hasn't.)

The first two sentences refer to real possibilities in the present and past. The forms can also be used to express unreal or untrue comparisons, as in the last three examples. Here the tenses are the same as those used in conditionals for hypothetical conditions in the present and past.

■ Complete the following sentences with phrases using **as if** or **as though** and appropriate verb forms.

1 He sounds _____ he (*know*) what he's talking about.
2 He speaks _____ he (*have*) a plum in his mouth.
3 The tourist asked me if I came from London, England, _____ I (*not know*) where London was.
4 He's retiring. It looks _____ he (*be tired*) of arguing with the rest of the managers.
5 Who do you think you are, ordering me about like that? You talk _____ you (*be*) the boss.
6 He looks so pleased with himself, _____ he (*say*) something clever instead of confusing the issue.

7 A Have you got hot and cold running water?
   B Of course we have. You talk _____ we (*live*) in the jungle.
8 At her wedding yesterday, the actress remarked, 'This is the love of my life', _____ she (*not been married*) six times before.

[10] 25
Conditional sentences

There are five basic combinations in Conditional sentences, all of which are familiar to you:

1 *If you **heat** water to 100°C, it **boils**.*

(General statement of permanent condition.)

2 *If the weather **is** good, we **will go** for a walk.*

(Specific situation.)

3 *If you **don't understand**, **ask** the teacher.*

(Imperative used instead of the Present Simple: a) in general terms, or instead of the Future Simple,   b) in a specific situation.)

4 *If I **knew** the answer, I **would tell** you.*

(Hypothetical, referring to the present or future. In fact, I don't know the answer.)

5 *If I **had known** the answer, I **would have told** you.*

(Hypothetical, referring to the past. In fact, I didn't know the answer, and so I couldn't tell you.)

Now study the variations on these combinations and note carefully the circumstances in which they are likely to be used.

Variations on 3 (above)

If you ***should happen*** *to meet him, please give him my kindest regards.*

(The introduction of **should** suggests that it is unlikely that you will meet him, although the possibility exists.)

Should you be *unable to contact him, come back to me for further instructions.*

(The inversion suggests that the possibility is even more remote, and in fact you are almost certain to be able to contact him.)

Variations on 4 (above)

*If we **were to offer** you the job, how soon would you be able to take it up?*

(The use of this form in place of **offered** suggests that the hypothetical offer of the job is still remote, or that the speaker wants to make it clear that there is no certainty that the job will be offered.)

Were we to offer you the job, how soon would you be able to take it up?

(Here, the hypothetical offer is so remote that it is very unlikely that it will be made.)

Variation on 5 (above)

Had I realised that you were coming, I would have met you at the station.

(This is simply a stylistic variation, found in more formal speech and writing.)

■ Rewrite the sentences below in the more familiar form you are used to in order to accustom yourself to the variations.

1   If you should happen to come across his address, please let me know.
2   Had we been consulted beforehand, we could have given you some good advice.
3   Should they try to prevent you from entering, show this pass.
4   Were they to protest, we would know how to handle the matter.
5   If I were to tell you what I really think, you would be horrified.
6   If he should speak to you about it, pretend that you don't know anything.
7   If the Headmaster were to hear about it, we would all be in trouble.
8   Had they given us any warning, we would have been able to get things ready in time.
9   Should you receive an alternative offer in the meantime, please let us know.
10 Had I been brought up in such conditions, I would probably have become a criminal, too.

Note   Other combinations are possible, but the only one you should note in particular is the polite form in which the conditional tense is used in both clauses:

I would be grateful if you *would let* me know how soon I can expect an answer to my letter.

[10] 26
Word order of adverbs of manner, place and time

While we cannot make absolute rules in these cases, the table indicates the normal order:

SUBJECT/VERB (OBJECT)	HOW	WHERE	WHEN
He works	*hard*	*in the garden*	*on Sundays.*

But when the verb is a verb of movement, for example, we are usually most interested in **where** someone is going, so the order is:

SUBJECT/VERB (OBJECT)	WHERE	HOW	WHEN
He returned	*home*	*as usual*	*in the evening.*

When there are a number of long adverbial phrases, or we want to emphasise the time, we can put the **when** adverbial at the beginning of the sentence:

WHEN	SUBJECT/VERB (OBJECT)	HOW	WHERE
As soon as he saw me	*he took me*	*hurriedly*	*inside.*

The same rule applies to sentences like those in the second group above.

Note that one-word adverbs of manner sometimes appear before the verb in sentences where they are emphasised, but not in the exercise below:

*She **hurriedly** closed the door. (She closed the door* ***hurriedly**.)*

■ Put the adverbial phrases (in brackets at the end of the sentence) into the most natural position in the sentence.

1   He travels (by train, every day, to London).
2   He listened (carefully, for a few moments, outside the door).
3   I'll read the report (after lunch, in detail, in my office).
4   They're coming (for a meeting, to the office, tomorrow).
5   They're planning to get married (at St Mary's Church, next week, quietly).
6   The bride arrived (at the church, in a Rolls-Royce, ten minutes before the service was due to begin).
7   We'll decide the matter (at the meeting, democratically, next week).
8   The guard stood (as soon as the officers came in sight, smartly, to attention).
9   They celebrated their victory (all through the night, in the street, joyfully).
10 He ate his lunch (alone, for the first time since he had got married, in the kitchen).

[10] 27

Verb + gerund, verb + infinitive

A Verb + gerund

Look at these sentences:

*I **enjoy working** here.*
*He **went on working** until he was 70.*

Enjoy is followed by a gerund. Other verbs that always take a gerund are: **admit, avoid, consider, delay, deny, detest, (can't) face, fancy, finish, (can't help, imagine, involve, keep (on), (not) mind, miss, practise, recollect, recommend, risk, (can't) stand** (see **hate** below), **suggest**. All verbs followed by a preposition (e.g. **go on**) take a gerund. (See Exercise 28 for verbs followed by the preposition **to** and a noun phrase or gerund but not the infinitive.)

- Make sentences of your own for each of the verbs listed above.

B Verb + gerund or infinitive with *to*

A number of verbs can take a gerund or an infinitive with **to**. In many cases the meaning changes depending on whether a gerund or an infinitive follows the verb. Here is a list of the most common verbs of this type:

allow *The doctor doesn't **allow me to smoke**.*
*We don't **allow smoking** in the classroom.*

Allow takes an infinitive when there is an object, e.g., **me**, but a gerund where there is none.

begin and *I'm **beginning/starting to feel** tired.*
start *I **began/started smoking** when I was fourteen.*

Begin and **start** are not normally found with a gerund in Continuous tenses.

continue *I **continued to write** to him.*
*I **continued writing** to him.*
hate *I **hate living** in London.*
*I'd **hate to live** on a boat.*

The gerund is the usual form, but the Conditional form, e.g., **I'd hate** is followed by the infinitive. Note also the use of the infinitive in expressions such as:

*I **hate/can't bear to interrupt** you when you're working.* (I'm sorry to interrupt you.)

Can't bear means the same as **hate** and may be followed by an infinitive, as in the example above, or a gerund; **can't stand** is always followed by a gerund.

intend *I **intend to visit** them.*
*I **intend visiting** them.*
like *I **like dancing**.*
*I **like to have** a good breakfast at weekends.*

The gerund is used in general statements, meaning 'enjoy', and the infinitive is used meaning 'prefer'. In the negative (when **don't like** means 'dislike'), **like** is followed by a gerund:

*I **don't like waiting** for buses.*

When **don't like** means 'I'm sorry to . . .' it is followed by the infinitive:

*I **don't like to disturb** you.*

In the Conditional, **like** takes the infinitive:

*I'd **like to help** you.*

love *I **love walking**.*
*I **love to stay** in bed late at weekends.*
The uses of **love** are the same as those of **like**.

prefer *I **prefer driving** to walking.*
*I **prefer to drive** rather than to walk.*

We use both the gerund and the infinitive after **prefer**, but the gerund form is easier to use and more idiomatic. The infinitive follows **I'd prefer** when we refer to a particular occasion:

*I'd **prefer to go** fishing rather than walking this Sunday.*

In this sense we often use **would rather** + infinitive without **to**:

*I'd **rather go** by car than walk this afternoon.*

regret *I **regret to tell** you that I have bad news.*
*I **regret telling** him all about the accident. It upset him.*

The infinitive is used to express regret in advance (about something we are going to say or do); the gerund is used to express regret afterwards (about something we have already said or done).

remember *I **remember smoking** my first cigarette.* (haven't forgotten)
*I **remembered to post** the letter.* (didn't forget)

We use **remember** + gerund after the event, **remember** + infinitive before the event.

Note that **recollect** takes the gerund (see **Verb + gerund** above); **remind**, meaning 'make someone remember' takes an object and the infinitive:

*He doesn't **recollect locking** the door.*
***Remind me to post** the letter.* (Don't let me forget.)

stop   *He **stopped talking**.* (He became silent.)
       *He **stopped** (in the street) **to talk** to a friend.*

The first example means 'he stopped what he was doing' (i.e. talking). The second example means 'he stopped walking because he wanted to talk to a friend'.

try   *I **tried to understand it**.* (I made the effort, I attempted.)
      *I **tried smoking** a cigar.* (I experimented, to see if I would like it.)

■ Study the examples given for verbs that can be followed by a gerund or an infinitive in different circumstances, and then complete the sentences in this exercise, using the correct form of the verb in brackets. If you think both gerund and infinitive forms are possible, say so.

1   We don't allow (smoke) in the classroom.
2   We don't allow students (smoke) in the classroom.
3   I began (learn) English several years ago.
4   Now I'm beginning (learn) Russian.
5   I shouted to him but he continued (walk) down the road without taking any notice.
6   I hate (work) at the weekend.
7   I hate (interrupt) classes when someone is teaching.
8   I'd hate (work) in a school like that.
9   I like (play) tennis.
10   I like (get up) early on Sunday mornings to go and play tennis.
11   I'd like (play) tennis tomorrow.
12   I like my opponents (hit) the ball hard, not just (try) to get it back.
13   I prefer (ride) a horse to a bicycle.
14   I'd rather (ride) a horse than a bicycle.
15   I regret (tell) you that your uncle has had an accident.
16   I regret (tell) her about it now. It caused her unnecessary pain.
17   Do you remember (see) a performance of *Hamlet* when you were about five?
18   *A* Did you remember (give) that message to Clara?
      B No, I forgot (tell) her. Why didn't you remind me (speak) to her when I went out this morning?
19   He never stops (talk). He must be an awful person to live with.
20   She's a very talkative woman. When she goes out shopping, she stops (talk) to everyone she meets.

21   *A* Have you ever tried (give up) smoking?
      B No. I've tried (smoke) a pipe instead of cigarettes, but I've never really tried (give up) altogether.
22   *A* Would you like me (see) you off at the airport tomorrow?
      B No, I'd rather (go) alone. I hate (say) goodbye to people. I start (worry) about the flight.

Note

Some verbs take the infinitive without **to**. These include **let, make** and most modals and auxiliaries, **can, must, would, had better, would rather,** etc. Exceptions are: **have to, ought to** and **used to**. But **be used to** and **get used to** take the gerund.

Help can take the infinitive with or without **to**:

*   **Help him (to) do it**.*

[10] 28

Verbs + preposition *to* + Noun phrase/ gerund

Notice the use of the gerund here after the main verb:

I look forward to your letter.
*I **look forward to hearing** from you.*

The following verbs are followed by the preposition **to** and by a noun phrase or gerund, but not by the infinitive: **amount to, be (get) accustomed to, be dedicated to, be devoted to, be given to, be opposed to, be (get) used to, come near to, limit oneself to, look forward to, object to, resign oneself to.**

■ Use verbs from the list above to complete these sentences. Do not use any verb more than once.

1   I don't see why I should _____ sitting in an armchair and doing nothing just because I'm over 60.
2   Don't take any notice of what he says. He's _____ making the wildest statements.
3   I _____ paying more for things than they are worth.
4   His whole life has been _____ caring for the sick.
5   Saying you have no opinion in the matter _____ taking the easy way out.
6   I _____ being criticised by people who don't understand me.
7   I've been _____ seeing you again ever since we met.
8   He was in such a bad temper that he _____ throwing something at me.

[11] 29

Indirect exclamations

Study the form and the word order of these sentences:

How tired I feel!
You've no idea how tired I feel.

What awful weather (we had)!
You can't imagine what awful weather we had.

What a beautiful present (she gave me)!
You'll never guess what a beautiful present she gave me.

Note that the word order in direct and indirect exclamations is the same.
Here are some less common examples of exclamations:

How people behave when they've had too much to drink!
What people will say when they lose their temper!
How much money people waste on silly things!

Such expressions are more commonly found, preceded by **It's amazing** . . ., **It's remarkable** . . ., **It's surprising** . . ., **It's astonishing** . . ., **It's incredible** . . ., etc.

■ Turn these sentences into indirect exclamations, using the correct form of exclamation, preceded by the phrase given in brackets:

He talked such nonsense. (You can't imagine)
You can't imagine what nonsense he talked.

1 We had such a wonderful time. (You can't imagine)
2 He's given me such a beautiful present. (You'll never guess)
3 I have to pay so much income tax. (It's incredible)
4 I was so pleased. (You can imagine)
5 It was such a boring party. (I can't begin to tell you)
6 The whole organisation was so inefficient. (He soon realised)
7 Some people are so greedy. (It's unbelievable)
8 The holiday cost us so little. (It's remarkable)

[11] 30

Have/get something done

Having something done suggests that someone is doing it for us. So instead of saying 'the barber is cutting his hair', we can say:

He is having his hair cut.

Get something done suggests more activity or effort:

I must go to the garage and get the car serviced.

■ In the following situations, suggest reasons why someone would make an appointment with the people listed:
To get the car overhauled.
Then suggest what sort of explanation someone else would give for his or her absence from home or from work:

He's having his car serviced.

1 She's at the hairdresser's.
2 He's at the optician's.
3 He's at the tailor's.
4 She's at the shoemaker's.
5 He's at the dentist's.
6 She's at home, with the decorators.
7 She's somewhere else in the office, in the photocopying room.
8 He's at the photographer's.

[11] 31

Separation of subject and main verb

Look at the subject and the main verb in these sentences:

His attitude, in my opinion, is quite unjustified.
Her father, who came with her, introduced her to us.
The girl, although she was shy, soon made friends.
Her brother, probably because he was rather aggressive, did not find it so easy.

When a subordinate clause or phrase occurs between commas in a sentence the subject is not repeated.
In some cases, students wrongly repeat a subject in a sentence without commas because they do not realise what the subject is:

The reason for it (subject) is that they have never troubled to find out what the workers want.
Whether or not you agree with me (subject) is of no importance to me.
That he should object to your behaving like that (subject) is quite understandable.

■ First include commas in the following passage to establish phrases and clauses in parenthesis, as shown above. Then use pronouns (**it, they,** etc.) in the spaces, where necessary.

Lie detectors are widely used in the United States to find out whether a person _____(1) is telling the truth or not. Polygraphers the people who operate them _____(2) claim that they can

30

establish guilt by detecting physiological changes that accompany emotional stress. Whether they will ever be adopted in Britian _____ (3) is a matter of opinion. Most people if they were given the chance to solve crimes simply by this method _____ (4) would probably think it was valuable but recent research not only raises doubts about how lie detectors _____ (5) should be used but also asks whether _____ (6) should be used at all. The reason it seems _____ (7) is that the tests apart from many of the polygraphers being unqualified _____ (8) are themselves capable of making mistakes. Perfectly innocent people with nothing to be afraid of _____ (9) often blush when a customs officer asks them questions. Fear which produces a heightened electrical response on the lie detector _____ (10) does not always establish guilt. It depends on whether the subject _____ (11) is afraid of being found out or _____ (12) is afraid of being wrongfully convicted. But a person whose past experience _____ (13) has prepared him for such tests _____ (14) can confuse the lie detector by reacting violently to neutral questions. So the lie detector although it may prove some people guilty _____ (15) will not always catch the criminal and _____ (16) may place innocent people under suspicion. It seems surprising that a much more effective way of using lie detectors which _____ (17) has been suggested by an American psychologist _____ (18) has not been put into practice more often. The method _____ (19) consists in asking the subject to read aloud certain statements about the crime when _____ (20) is connected to the lie detector. Anyone who is unaware of the true facts _____ (21) would make no distinction between saying 'the thieves used a red car' and 'the thieves used a blue car'. But a person who was involved in the crime although he tried to disguise his reaction _____ (22) might give himself away. That an innocent person could be convicted because of the evidence of a machine _____ (23) is the most serious accusation that can be made against lie detectors and this possibility if the psychologist's method were used _____ (24) would be avoided.

[13] 32
Used to, be used to, would

Look at the following sentences:

*When I was at school, I **used to** study every night* (but now I go out and have a good time).
*I **used not to/didn't use to** smoke when I was at school* (but now I smoke 20 cigarettes a day).
*I'm **used to** getting up early. I've been doing it for years.*
*He **wasn't used to** washing his own clothes. His mother had always done it for him.*
*Whenever Uncle Charles came to visit us, he **would** bring a present for all the children.*

Used to is a past form contrasting with the present to express what we habitually did, but do not do now. The negative form is **used not to** or **didn't use to. Used to** is always followed by an infinitive.
We can use the Past Simple to express the same idea, but this does not contrast past and present actions:
*I **studied** hard when I was at school* (and I'm still studying hard now that I am at university).
We use the Present Simple, not **used to**, to express what we habitually do in the present:
I smoke 20 cigarettes a day.
Be used to can be used with any tense of the verb **be. Used** means 'accustomed'; it indicates a habit formed by experience. **Be used to** is always followed by a gerund or a noun.
Would is used for a repeated action in the past. It is most commonly used in the main clause of a sentence when the subordinate clause begins with **whenever** or **every time**. When we say, 'he used to do something', this implies that he doesn't do that thing now. When we say, 'he would do something', we are only talking about an action repeated in the past, which may or may not still happen in the present.

■ Complete the sentences below with **used to, be used to** or **would** and the verb given in brackets; use **would** whenever possible.

1 I (play) tennis quite well, but I haven't been able to play since Christmas.
2 He wasn't nervous, in spite of the large audience, because he (gave) lectures.
3 I (live) in the country, before we moved here.
4 My parents often (visit) us while we were there.
5 Whenever they came down, they (remark) on the freshness of the air. I suppose we (breathe) it so we took it for granted. But every time they got into the car to say 'goodbye', they (look) wistfully around them, as if they were sorry to go.
6 I (work) quite hard, but now I take it easy.
7 I (be) hard work, and my wife (work) hard, too.
8 My grandfather (say) things like that, when I was a boy. Every time he came to see us, he (make) a speech about hard work. It (get) on my nerves, I can tell you.

[13] 33

Prepositional relative clauses

Compare these sentences:

*The room **where/in which my grandfather was born** is kept as a museum.*
*This room, **where/in which my grandfather was born**, is kept as a museum.*

In prepositional clauses of this kind, whether they are defining (first example) or non-defining (second example), the preposition with **which** can be used as an alternative to **where**. However, note that it would be possible in the first case to write:

*The room **my grandfather was born in** is kept as a museum.*

This is less formal in style.

Note, on the other hand, that we cannot substitute a prepositional clause for the relative adverb **where** when a specific place is mentioned by name:

*This system has been tried out in Spain, **where** it has already achieved considerable success.*
*Next week I am going to **Cheshire, where** my cousin lives.*

In most sentences of this kind, **where** can be substituted for a prepositional clause:

*The company **of which (where) he is the manager** (or the company **he is manager of**) made a big profit last year.*
*The XYZ company, **of which (where) he is the manager**, made a big profit last year.*

This is only impossible in cases where 'place' is not involved:

*The fund **of which he is the principal trustee** is responsible for helping children.*

■ Replace the prepositional clauses with **which** in the following passages with clauses using **where**, or with clauses which have the preposition at the end. Indicate those sentences or clauses where the use of **which** is incorrect.

1   Last week, I went to Amsterdam, (1) at which there is a superb collection of pictures by Van Gogh. The museum (2) in which the pictures are housed has a lot of interesting information about the houses (3) in which he lived, the area (4) in which he worked as a kind of worker priest, and the South of France, (5) in which he died.

2   He found it difficult to find a publisher for his first novel, (6) of which he was very proud. The company (7) to which he sent it asked to see him, however. They wanted to know if the places (8) about which he had written, and in particular his native village, (9) in which most of his novel took place, were the only topics

(10) with which he could deal. 'The point is.' said the publisher, 'that this company, (11) of which I am the manager, is interested in the American market, (12) in which books with an English background are not so popular.'

[14] 34

Complex tenses in future time clauses

The following combinations will already be familiar:

*As soon as I **get** home, I'**ll ring** him.*
*I'm going to **have** a party **when** the examinations **are** over.*
***Raise** the flag when I **give** you the signal.*
*He **may not know** what to do **until** he **hears** from you.*
*I **won't be able to confirm** the dates until I **can talk** to the manager.*

In all of these examples, the Present tense is used in the part of the time clause containing the time expression (**when, until**, etc.) while the main clause may be in the Future (**will, going to**) but can also be formed with the imperative or **may**, for example.

Now look at these examples:

*When I'**ve spoken** to the manager, I'**ll know** what to do.*

The Present Perfect tense can take the place of a Present tense here when it refers to a completed action.

You're lucky to be going on holiday at this time of year.
*While we're **sweating** in the office, you'**ll be lying** on the beach.*

The Continuous forms are used in both clauses to indicate two actions going on at the same time in the future.

*By the time we **get** there, the film **will have started**.*

The Future Perfect tense, instead of the Future Simple, indicates that the film will start before they get there, so that when they arrive, they will say: 'The film **has started**'.

■ Complete the following sentences, using an appropriate verb in the correct tense.

1   July 10th is my wedding anniversary. Next month, my husband and I _____ for twenty years.

2   While you're ringing, I _____ anxiously to hear what she says.

3   When you _____ the washing-up, will you put the plates away, please?

4   He takes so long to decide what he is going to eat. By the time he has made up his mind (completed action), we _____ a whole bottle of wine.

5 Jimmy will come out to play when he _____ his homework.
6 By the time they reach an agreement over the strike, everyone _____ what it was about in the first place.

_____ child could have done it. In fact, _____ children paint a good deal better. _____ bought that for the museum must have been mad.
A It's very valuable, _____ you think.

[14] 35

Any, anyone, some, someone, whatever, whoever

Compare these sentences:

Any contribution you make will be welcome. (It doesn't matter how much.)
You ought to make some contribution to the cause. (A certain amount.)
Whatever you contribute will go to a good cause. (Anything.)
Anyone who thinks that is crazy. (It doesn't matter who he/she is.)
If you know someone who thinks that, then he must be crazy. (A particular person.)
Whoever said that was crazy. ('The person who . . .', it doesn't matter who he/she was.)

■ Complete these sentences with **any, anyone, some, someone, whatever** or **whoever**.

1 A There's _____ at the door.
   B Well, I'm not going to let him in, _____ he is.
2 It's easy to criticise. _____ can do that. What we need is _____ who will make constructive suggestions.
3 A I'm only trying to give you _____ useful advice.
   B I'm going to do what I like, _____ you say.
   A I should have thought _____ advice was better than none in your situation.
4 A _____ who wants to attend the concert should contact me for tickets.
   B I know _____ who wants to go.
   A Well, _____ it is, ask him to see me.
5 A This calculator will provide the answer to _____ mathematical problem. You can ask it _____ you like.
   B I don't believe it. There must be _____ questions it can't answer.
6 A In _____ serious work of art, the artist, _____ he is, has _____ clear intention in his mind when he begins to paint.
   B Really? Well, look at that painting over there. It looks like an old piece of cardboard.

[14] 36

Verbs taking the subjunctive

A demand, insist, propose, suggest, recommend

These are the most common of a group of verbs which take a clause with **that** and the subjunctive (**should**) after them.

'Let's take a vote on it!' James said.
James proposed that they should take a vote on it.

■ Rewrite the following sentences in reported speech, using the most appropriate of these verbs to introduce the sentence.

1 'No, no, please! You mustn't go until you've seen the photographs,' Harold said.
2 'Why don't you show them to us the next time we come?' said Paula.
3 'The workers must get a pay rise of 12%,' said the shop steward.
4 'Let's take the matter to arbitration,' said the chairman.
5 'It would be a good idea if everyone kept calm,' said the accountant.

B ask, authorise, command, order, require, urge

Some verbs can be used with this construction, but if there is a personal object, they are more often followed by the object and infinitive:

The inspector ordered that the suspect should be detained.
The inspector ordered his men to detain the suspect.

■ Rewrite the following sentences in reported speech, using the most appropriate of these verbs to introduce the sentence. Use the object and infinitive construction in all cases.

1 'Please can I stay up to watch the horror film?' Alice said to her mother. (Use 'let'.)
2 'This document allows you to leave the country,' the official told him.
3 'Keep trying!' the manager shouted to the players.

4 'Don't shoot till you see the whites of their eyes,' the old soldier told his comrades.

5 'The rules say that you must sign this in triplicate,' the clerk said to me.

6 'Treat the prisoner well,' the colonel told the jailers.

[17] 37

Need and needn't

A Compare these sentences:

*Does he really **need to leave** so soon?* (or ***Need he leave** . . .?*)

*Is it really **necessary for** him **to leave** so soon?*

■ Change the sentences below from one construction to the other.
1 Does he really need to work so hard?
2 Is it really necessary for him to spend so much money?
3 Need you take so many clothes with you?
4 They don't need to pay immediately.
5 It isn't necessary for us to book in advance.
6 You needn't come, if you don't want to.

B   Past forms of *needn't*

Compare these sentences:

*I **didn't need to go** to school yesterday because it was a holiday.* (As a result, I didn't go.)

*You **needn't have done** the washing-up this evening. We could have left it until tomorrow.* (But in fact you did it, even though it was not necessary.)

■ Change the sentences below into forms using the past of **needn't** in one of these two constructions. Decide first of all whether you think the person did the action or not.
1 You paid more than was necessary for the house. (Use 'so much'.)
2 In the end, it wasn't necessary for me to ring him, because he called to see me.
3 It wasn't necessary for you to have bought so much bread. Now we'll have to throw some of it away.
4 It rained hard yesterday. It was a good thing it wasn't necessary for me to go shopping.
5 They had already arranged to spend the night at a friend's house, so it wasn't necessary for us to put them up.
6 The food wasn't very good, but he made a quite unnecessary fuss about it. (Use 'such'.)

[17] 38

Fairly, quite, rather

A   *quite, rather*

Compare these sentences:

*She's **quite** tall.*
*She's **rather** short.*
*She's **rather** (too) tall to be a ballet dancer.*

In general, we use **quite** to mean 'comparatively' when we are in favour of something and **rather** when we are more critical of it. Both words can be used to qualify adjectives and adverbs, but only **rather** can be used with **too**. Most people think it is a good thing to be tall, so **quite tall** is positive where **rather short** sounds negative.
On the other hand, a tall ballet dancer may find it difficult to get a partner of her height, so in these circumstances it is a disadvantage to be tall, and we use **rather (too) tall**.

■ Complete these sentences with **quite** or **rather**.
1 The trains to London are _____ frequent but they sometimes arrive _____ late.
2 She played _____ well, although she began the game _____ nervously.
3 The air is hot and sticky outside but it's _____ cool in the house.
4 I feel _____ cold. I'm going to put the central heating on.
5 The sun's _____ warm. You should get a lovely tan.
6 The sun's _____ too hot for me. I'm going into the shade.
7 The children are _____ polite although of course they're _____ noisy, like most children.
8 A You look _____ tired.
   B Yes, I've had a _____ tiring day, though it was _____ enjoyable.

B   *fairly, rather*

Compare these sentences:

A What was the food like?
*B **Fairly** good, though we ate better at the other restaurant last night.*
A What was the food like?
*B It was **rather** good, actually, though the restaurant looked very ordinary from the outside.*

Fairly also means 'comparatively (good), but not as good as one hoped or expected'. **Rather** can mean 'better than expected', when it is used with favourable adjectives or adverbs.

- Complete these sentences with **fairly** or **rather**.

  1 I'm _____ confident about the exam, though I won't feel happy about it until I see the papers.
  2 I was sure I'd fail the exam, but now that I've done the papers I feel confident I've passed. I did most of the questions _____ well.
  3 The job's _____ straightforward, though there are a few things that worry me about it.
  4 I've always thought she was ugly, but today she looked _____ attractive.
  5 I didn't like him at first, but in the end I became _____ fond of him.
  6 *A* How do you feel?
    B _____ well, but I don't think I'd better get up yet.
  7 *A* How do you feel?
    B You know, it's surprising, but I feel _____ energetic, in spite of working all day.

C   *rather* + comparative

Look at these sentences:

*Unfortunately, he was **rather** fatter than I remember him.*
*The book was **rather** more interesting than its cover suggested.*

Only **rather** can be used with comparative forms, whether the adjective or adverb carries a good or bad meaning.

- Look again at the difference between **quite** and **rather** in Section A; then use **quite** or **rather** to complete the following sentences.

  1 He was _____ well this morning, but since lunch his condition has become _____ more serious.
  2 It's _____ a good novel, _____ better constructed than his last one.
  3 This year's sales figures were _____ disappointing. We hope to sell _____ more next year.
  4 The play was _____ good but it lasted _____ longer than necessary, and some of the audience got _____ bored towards the end.
  5 She's _____ a good student but she got _____ nervous when the exam began, and did _____ worse than I had expected.

D   *quite* meaning 'absolutely'

Look at these sentences:

*The performance was **quite** extraordinary.*
*I'm sorry. That's **quite** impossible.*

Quite can mean 'absolutely, completely, perfectly, totally', when it is used to modify absolute adjectives, such as superb, dead, horrible, black.

- Use **quite** or **fairly** to complete the following sentences. Use **fairly** when you think the meaning is 'comparatively', although you must remember that **quite** could be used in all cases.

  1 *A* Are you _____ sure that that's right?
    B Yes, absolutely certain.
  2 His explanation was _____ convincing, though I'd like to hear what the other witnesses have to say before I make up my mind.
  3 You know _____ well that I would never do anything to upset her.
  4 *A* He seemed to think the price was _____ reasonable though he's obviously looking for something cheaper.
    B But that's _____ ridiculous. He'd never get anything cheaper than that.
  5 We had _____ good weather. At least it was better than last year. Last year, it was _____ appalling, It rained all the time.
  6 *A* He's _____ reliable.
    B I don't think you're being fair to him. He's _____ as reliable as the man we had before.
  7 *A* I've never seen anything _____ like it.
    B Oh, really. I thought that sort of occurrence was _____ common here.
  8 *A* The situation looks _____ encouraging.
    B I don't agree with you. I can't see anything good about it. It seems _____ hopeless to me.

[17] 39

Specially and *especially*

Compare these sentences:

*It often rains here, **especially** in winter.*
*It's always cold, but it's **especially** cold in winter.*
*The house has been **specially** designed to keep out the cold.*
*I'm interested in everything on display but I'm **especially** interested in the new central heating system.*

Especially means 'particularly' and is the adverb most commonly used, although the only form of adjective found nowadays is **special**. **Specially** is used as in the third example above with a past participle form to indicate that something was done for a particular purpose or for a particular person. Consequently, we find it in combinations like **specially made, specially built, specially written,** etc. But there are cases (as in the fourth example above) where a past participle is employed but this meaning is not intended, and then **especially** would be used.

- Complete these sentences with **specially** or **especially**.

1 It gets very hot here, _____ in summer.
2 This summer has been _____ hot, much warmer than usual.
3 *A* This sunshade is _____ made to keep the sun off but not to blow away.
   B Don't you call that an awning?
   A No, an awning is _____ designed for shops. It helps to keep the shop cool and protect the passers-by from the sun. They're often brightly coloured, _____ outside cafes.
4 He was anxious to track down the band of criminals and _____ concerned to arrest the leader. Consequently he employed a group of men _____ trained for the task, since he was afraid that the criminals would use violence, _____ if they were surrounded and could see no way out.
5 The music has been _____ composed for the film and adds a great deal to the effect, _____ in the final scene.

[19] 40
Use and omission of the definite article

Use the examples given below for reference. There is also an exercise devoted to this topic in *Book 1* of this course, Unit 19, page 110. The exercise on page 110 is to be attempted if further practice is required.

A Omission of *the*

We do not use **the** with the following:

1 Games and sports

   *I **play football** every week. My sister is **good at tennis** and **fond of swimming**, too.*

2 Subjects of study

   *I **studied literature** at university; my brother **studied physics**.*

3 Languages

   *Many Welsh people **speak Welsh** but most Scots **speak English**.*

Note that we can say **the English** (noun) or **English people**, but nationality as an adjective has no definite or indefinite article:
   I'm English.

4 Meals and clock times

   *A What time do you **have breakfast**?*
   *B **About eight o'clock**.*

5 Gerunds

   ***Horse racing** is more popular in Britain than **fox-hunting**.*

6 Collocations (preposition + noun)

Notice that there is no **the** after the prepositions in these sentences:

   *A Is Maureen still **in bed**?*
   *B No, she went **to work** early this morning.*

A number of common phrases in English, made up of a preposition and a noun, do not take **the**.
Here is a list of the most common ones:
bed (**in, to**)
church (**at, in** = inside, **to**)
court (**in, to**)
dock (**in**)
harbour (**in**)
home (**at**)
hospital (**in, to**)
market (**at, to**)
paper (**on**)
prison (**in, to**)
school (**at, to**)
sea (**at, to**)
university (**at, to**)
work (**at, to**)

The definite article is only used when we clearly refer to a particular school, hospital, etc:

   *He **left school** at eighteen and went **to university**.*
   *I'm not teaching **at the school** today. I'm going **to the university**.*

Modes of travel and transport take **by** + noun, without **the**:
   *We decided to do the journey **by air/sea/road**.*
   *I prefer travelling **by car/bus/plane/train**.*
Note that we say **on foot**.

B Use of *the*

We use **the** with the following:

1 Weights and measures

   *Petrol is sold **by the litre**.*

2 Musical instruments

   *A Can you play **the piano**?*
   *B No, but I used to learn **the violin**.*

3 Groups or classes of people

> **The young** *often get impatient with their parents*.

We can say either **the young** or **young people**. The verb that follows expressions of this kind is plural.

4 Rivers, seas, mountain ranges

> **The Amazon** *is longer than* **the River Thames**.
> **The Mediterranean** *flows into* **the Atlantic Ocean**.
> **Mount Everest** *is the highest mountain in* **the Himalayas**.

Note that we use **the** in all cases, except for the name of a single mountain:

> *e.g.* **Mount Everest, Kilimanjaro**.

5 Unique objects, points of the compass, some time expressions

> **The earth** *goes round* **the sun**.

We use **the** when there is only one of something, e.g., **the sun, the moon, the earth, the world**. We use **the** with points of the compass, e.g., **the north, the south, the east, the west**. But compare these sentences:

> *We were travelling* **north**.
> *We were travelling* **towards the north**.

We usually use **the** when we speak of **the past, the present** and **the future**. The exceptions are **at present** which means 'now, at this time' and **in future** which means 'from now on':

> *I'll drive more carefully* **in future**. (From now on, from this moment.)
> **In the future** (but not from now on) *men may live on the moon*.

C Use and omission of *the*

A good rule to remember is:

we use **the** when we are talking about something specific;
we don't use **the** when we are speaking in a more general sense.

1 Plural count nouns and mass nouns

> *She likes* **flowers**. (general)
> *She liked* **the flowers** *that I gave her*. (specific)
> **Coffee** *is expensive nowadays*. (general)
> **The coffee** *that you bought is very bitter*. (specific)

2 Abstract nouns

> *I always admire* **honesty**. (general)
> *I was surprised at* **the honesty** *with which he answered the questions*. (specific)

3 Species of animals

> **Elephants** *are said to have long memories*.

When we talk about animals in general, we usually use the plural without **the**. When we refer to a particular species we can use either.**the** and a singular noun or a plural noun without **the**.

> **The Indian elephant is smaller than the African elephant.**
> **Indian elephants are smaller than African elephants.**

Note that we say **Man, mankind**, but **the human race.**

4 Noun + modifying phrase/clause

> **Life** *is worth living*.
> **Modern life** *is often tiring*.
> **Albert Schweitzer's life** *was devoted to the sick*.
> **Life in Britain** *today is very different from* **life in the nineteenth century**.
> **The life he is leading** *bores him*.
> **The life of a typical salesman** *today can be very tiring*.
> **The life of Albert Schweitzer** *is an example to everyone*.
> **The life of our ancestors** *was very different from* **the life we lead today**

The is used when the noun is modified by a relative clause, or by a phrase including **of**.

■ Complete the passage, putting **the** in the spaces where it is necessary.

_____(1) life in _____(2) modern world is easier in some ways than _____(3) life our grandparents lived. Advances in _____(4) technology have made it more comfortable. We have only to compare _____(5) convenience of _____(6) travelling by _____(7) air to _____(8) long journeys by _____(9) land and _____(10) sea that were common a hundred years ago.
In particular, _____(11) medical science has done a great deal to combat _____(12) disease. _____(13) terrible problems of _____(14) childbirth, for example, are almost a thing of _____(15) past. But _____(16) life we lead today has its disadvantages, too. _____(17) present generation of _____(18) parents has grown up in _____(19) shadow of _____(20) war and we all share _____(21) concern experts feel about _____(22) pollution and _____(23) disappearance of _____(24) world's natural resources.

_____(25) modern parents are worried that _____(26) young, their children, will not inherit _____(27) perfect world that _____(28) optimists of _____(29) technological revolution prophesied at _____(30) beginning of _____(31) twentieth century.

In _____(32) situation that faces us, it's no use _____(33) playing _____(34) fiddle while _____(35) Rome burned, as Nero, _____(36) Roman emperor, did, or _____(37) playing _____(38) golf at _____(39) weekend, while _____(40) poor and _____(41) unemployed starve, which is _____(42) modern equivalent of it in _____(43) Western society. We have to work together to build _____(44) kind of _____(45) future that our children should have. _____(46) building it will probably require _____(47) sacrifice and _____(48) unselfishness on _____(49) part of _____(50) richer nations of _____(51) world, as well as _____(52) intelligence and _____(53) ingenuity.

[19] 41
Inversion: *Only*

You have already seen a number of examples of the inversion of the verb form when the sentence begins with certain words, primarily with negative adverbs. See Exercises 81, 83 and 84 (pages 67 and 68). There are also a number of words that count as negative in such cases, such as **hardly, rarely, scarcely, seldom**. The most deceptive is **only**, since not all sentences beginning with this word require the inversion of the verb form.

Compare these sentences:

> **Only Harold completed** the test satisfactorily.
> **Only when he had finished did he realise** that he had made several mistakes.

Only counts as a negative adverb at the beginning of a sentence if it modifies the verb and the verb form is inverted (**did he realise**). This is not the case if it qualifies the noun (**Harold**).

- Complete the following sentences by inserting **only** at the beginning and change the verb form, inverting it where necessary:

1 a The person who wears the shoe knows if it fits him.
  b You find out if a shoe fits you by wearing it. (Begin: 'Only by wearing . . .')

2 a His closest friend knew what had happened.
  b He discovered what had happened by asking his closest friends. (Begin: 'Only by asking . . .')
3 a When she grew up, Sarah understood how important the meeting had been.
  b Sarah understood how important the meeting had been.
4 a A first-class writer could have written this novel.
  b As the novel develops, we discover what its real meaning is.
5 a Northerners speak like that.
  b In the north people speak like that.

[19] 42
Inversion: *No sooner*

The problem with this expression is that you must remember that it is Comparative in form, apart from the fact that if it begins the sentence the verb form must be inverted. Study these sentences and compare them:

> She **had no sooner entered** the room **than** she realised something was missing.
> **No sooner had** she **entered** the room **than** she realised something was missing.

Of course, there is a much simpler way of writing the sentence and conveying the same meaning:

> **As soon as** she **entered** the room, she realised something was missing.

- Change the examples below from the construction given to each of the other two.

1 I had no sooner received your telegram than I contacted the agency.
2 No sooner had I completed one book than I had to begin another.
3 As soon as the money was paid, the prisoner was released.
4 I had no sooner arrived at the beach than it started to rain.
5 No sooner had they sold the house than they were offered a better price for it.

Section 2: Passages for comprehension and summary

[3] 00

■ Read the following passage carefully.

A Space in the Country

A green revolution has been taking place in the countryside. But so quietly has it been carried out, and with so little fuss, that many people are unaware of what has been achieved. Don't expect to find anything so wild or so big as a national park, or anything as small and tame as your local rec. Country parks come somewhere between the two, with the accent on leisure rather than conservation.

Ten years ago the country park was nothing more than an idea floated in a Government White Paper called *Leisure in the Countryside*. Today there are well over 100 country parks flourishing in nearly every corner of England and Wales, and more parks are in the pipeline.

They were designed to serve three basic purposes: to make it easier for town dwellers to enjoy the open air without travelling too far and adding to traffic congestion; to ease the pressure on the more remote and solitary places; and above all, perhaps, in the words of the White Paper, to 'reduce the risk of damage to the countryside – aesthetic, as well as physical – which often comes about when people simply settle down for an hour or a day where it suits them, somewhere "in the country" – to the inconvenience and indeed the expense of the countryman who lives there.'

A good country park will certainly be readily accessible for cars and pedestrians and you may be able to reach it by public transport. It will cover at least 25 acres and may contain woods, open parkland or a stretch of water. It may even be on the coast.

Some country parks provide refreshment facilities, picnic sites, information centres and a warden service. All of them have car parks and toilets. There may be an admission fee or a charge for parking your car, and a few parks close during the winter, so it is best to check before setting out. The great thing about country parks is that they are prepared for people. So you feel really welcome in the countryside.

In some parks you can swim, sail, fish, row or go horse-riding. Others offer quieter pleasures: nature trails, gardens, ancient monuments, fine views.

The commonest type of park is the traditional parkland of some bygone ancestral estate, sometimes with the great house or castle still intact within the grounds, as at Elvaston Castle, near Derby. But there is no truly typical country park. In landscape terms their range is immense: downs, cliffs, woods, moors, heaths – even reclaimed mineral workings, old gravel pits and derelict railway lines have been transformed with the aid of cash handouts from the Countryside Commission.

A few private individuals and non-public bodies such as the National Trust have established country parks, but so far most country parks have been set up by local authorities. Nevertheless the picture as a whole is bright. A survey carried out last year by the Countryside Commission showed that on one Sunday in July well over 200,000 people visited the parks. Whatever other change may alter the face of the countryside in coming decades, one thing is certain. Country parks are here to stay.

The questions asked on passages like this in the Use of English paper are of three kinds. First, there are general comprehension questions, like numbers 4, 9, 11 and 14 in the exercise below. You may be used to answering such questions in multiple-choice format, but here it is essential that you should write out your answer in good English. The answer should be one, or in some cases two, sentences. It is a good idea to develop the habit from the beginning of writing complete sentences. For example, it would be possible to begin the answer to question 4: 'Because . . .', but it is preferable to write 'It is likely because . . .'. The instructions do not specifically state that you should answer in your own words, and it is certainly unwise to reword sentences completely in order to avoid the phrasing used in the text. It is good practice, however, for summary writing and for your English in general to answer naturally in your own words as far as you can. In some cases, though not in the questions mentioned here, it may be possible to answer a question with a quotation from the text, but in that case you should indicate that this is not just a lucky guess by writing the answer within inverted commas, like this:
" . . . ."

Secondly, you may be asked to explain the meaning of a word or phrase, as in the first three questions below. Once again, it is wise to write a complete sentence: 'It means . . .' (remembering the 's' on the third person singular form!). Try to define the phrase as completely as you can. For instance, if you write as an answer to the first question: 'It means a change', you are indicating that you understand the word 'revolution', but not that you understand the kind of revolution that is taking place. A valid answer would be: 'It means a change taking place in the countryside because of the establishment of country parks.'

The third kind of question, such as number 5 below, is really grammatical. It is to test whether you understand the relationship of words and sentences to those that precede or follow them. 'It' must normally (but not always) refer to what has gone before. Does this 'It' refer to 'public transport' or is it necessary to go back further to find the phrase concerned? The meaning of the sentences as a whole should indicate the correct answer.

[3] 43

■ Now answer the following questions on the passage.

1 What is meant by 'a green revolution' (line 1)?
2 What is meant by 'with the accent on leisure rather than conservation' (lines 7–8)?
3 What is meant by 'in the pipeline' (lines 13–14)?
4 Why is it likely that people who settle down for an hour or a day will cause the countryman inconvenience and expense?
5 What does 'It' refer to in line 29?
6 What should you check before setting out (line 37)?
7 And what does 'setting out' mean?
8 What does 'bygone' mean in line 45?
9 Why is there no truly typical country park (line 48)?
10 What does 'their' refer to in line 49?
11 How have the Countryside Commission helped the country parks scheme?
12 Why was this necessary?
13 What does 'the picture as a whole is bright' mean in lines 57–8?
14 What is the evidence for this?
15 What does 'country parks are here to stay' mean in line 63?

[3] 44

Later in this book you will be asked to summarise the main points made in an article like this in a paragraph of your own of about 100 words. Read the explanation that follows carefully so that you will be able to handle this sort of question. Here the question would be: 'Explain why country parks were set up and why they attract so many people.'

Stage 1 Read the passage two or three times (for about ten minutes).

Stage 2 Make notes on it, trying to express the main points in your own words.

From a careful reading, you should have realised that some parts of the text are more relevant to the question than others. For example, the first two sentences do not tell us anything about the reasons for setting up country parks, only that many people do not know that there are so many. You should also bear in mind that you have only 100 words to express the ideas contained in the passage (about 10 lines on this page). You cannot afford to waste words on details and lists of different things – for example, all the different facilities the parks offer (lines 32–43) or the different types of landscape (lines 44–53). When making notes, try to think of a phrase or sentence which will express such details in general terms.

The notes you have made might look something like this:

1 Country parks set up in the last 10 years.
2 Reasons – a) to help town dwellers to enjoy countryside without having to go far away
   b) to protect more remote places from too many visitors
   c) to protect interests of country people from careless, irresponsible visitors.
3 Parks are easy to reach, quite large.
4 Different kinds of countryside.
5 Facilities prepared to help people enjoy themselves and be comfortable.
6 Variety of interesting things to do.
7 Very popular with the public.

Note that I have deliberately left out the lists, summarising them in Points 4 and 6, and have not explained which authorities are involved in setting up different parks. This is not part of the question.

Stage 3 Write a first draft of your summary from your notes – *not* from the original, otherwise it will be too long and look like a selection of sentences, not a summary. Where possible, join your points together in a logical way. It is not essential that they should always appear in the same order, though you will find it easier if they do on most occasions.

The first draft may look like this:

Over 100 country parks have been set up in England and Wales in the last ten years. This has been done mainly to help people living in towns to enjoy the countryside without having to go far away. They also protect wild nature spots and the country and country people from careless, irresponsible visitors. The parks are within easy reach of towns and offer different kinds of countryside to visitors, so none of them is typical. Everything has been done to provide facilities for visitors which will help them to enjoy themselves in comfortable surroundings. There are usually plenty of interesting things to do and so the parks have become very popular with the public. (115 words)

Stage 4 You will usually find that you have written rather more than is required. You must try to cut down the draft to 100 words, without wasting too much time on counting words exactly and without spoiling the English.

Aim first at unnecessary adjectives and details (in brackets in the example below). I have left out thirteen words, so the total is 102, which is sufficient for the purpose. If I had needed further cuts, I would have looked for ways of saying the same thing in fewer words. Here, for example, I could write 'near' instead of 'within easy reach of' and 'Facilities are provided' instead of 'Everything has been done to provide facilities'. taking out eleven words and using four.

(Over 100) Country parks have been set up in England and Wales in the last ten years, (This has been done mainly) to help people living in towns to enjoy the countryside without having to go far away. They also protect (wild nature spots and) the country and country people from (careless) irresponsible visitors. The parks are within easy reach of towns and offer different kinds of countryside to visitors, so none of them is typical. Everything has been done to provide facilities for visitors which will help them to enjoy themselves in comfortable surroundings. There are usually plenty of interesting things to do and so the parks have become (very) popular with the public.

Stage 5 Rewrite the finished summary.
Although the technique I am suggesting may seem difficult at first, in my experience it is the only way in which a foreign student can write a summary which is still readable English but is not a copy of sentences in the original. Bear in mind, however, that it is not a good policy to begin cutting too soon or to cut more than is necessary. If you do so, the English will become a number of short, unrelated sentences, and you will almost certainly leave out essential information as well as unnecessary details.

Refer back to this example in future lessons when you are asked to write a summary until you have got used to the technique.

[4] 00

- Read the following passage carefully.

Cost and Compassion

Within the next few days, the British Government will announce whether it intends to give those disabled people already qualified to drive powered vehicles either a weekly 'mobility' allowance or some form of modified four-wheel car. What is certain is that the three-wheeler will no longer be issued, and the scandalous list of unnecessary deaths and injuries it has caused to already
5   handicapped people can now be closed.

    The arguments about the propriety or feasibility of helping disabled people to live fuller and more independent lives have always been complicated, because they tend to mix up ethics and technology. The solutions proposed, therefore, never seem satisfactory, because they cannot provide a single answer to either aspect. If the state did not admit any obligation to provide a
10   degree of care for the handicapped that included assistance with transport, then discussions could centre on moral, ethical, or political principles. But these questions have already been answered implicitly. The State accepts the obligation; the question that has remained is how to discharge it.

    It has been government policy for many years to provide a three-wheeled petrol- or battery-driven car, known as a tricycle, for those people with sufficient ability to handle simple
15   controls and react adequately to other traffic. Despite the illusion that its three-point support gives stability, the tricycle has been shown to be more unstable than four-wheelers. In the year 1973–74, more than 250 of the most up-to-date models overturned, and there are over 1,600 injured drivers whose claims for compensation are still pending.

    The rising number of complaints and accidents resulting solely from the bad design of the
20   vehicle has prodded various governments into (a) denying that it was unsafe, (b) admitting it was unsafe but pleading it was the best solution available, and (c) withdrawing the right of the disabled to the tricycle. This latter decision is the one currently under review. Yet there are comparatively cheap and technically sound solutions already available to this problem. Of course, with adequate funds almost any degree of handicap can be met, but without going far beyond the existing
25   allocation, the 21,000 people at present driving tricycles could be supplied with vehicles as safe as the four-wheeled equivalents.

    What appears to be an economic difficulty is that the low number of drivers involved does not provide a sufficiently large market for the benefits of mass production. But this is a problem of concept rather than fact. A city car and one for the disabled have many requirements in common.
30   These include low fuel consumption, cheap servicing, simple controls, small dimensions, and low cruising speeds. There is a mass market for a car along these lines, and, once established, careful design at the planning stage could make optional variations for the disabled cheap to incorporate. For example, a conventional car with its passenger door hinged at the bottom rather than at the side greatly modifies the problem of access of someone who has to transfer from a wheelchair to a
35   driver's seat. Again, variomatic drive (now common in many cars) eliminates the difficulties of changing gear.

    Not only would a mass-produced car offer financial relief to a government with limited resources; it might even provide a market for an industry now beset with problems of under-employment and diminishing markets. Certainly, the alternative of a weekly grant is a
40   compromise that makes the worst of the available options. In the long run it will be expensive, it will be inadequate, and it will not meet the need of many handicapped people.

[4] 45

■ Answer the following questions on the passage.

1 What is the Government now proposing to offer disabled people, and why?

2 What is the significance of the use of the word 'already' in the phrase 'already handicapped' (lines 4–5)?

3 Why can the 'list' referred to in line 4 now be closed?

4 What does 'they' refer to in line 8?

5 What does 'admit' mean in line 9?

6 What does 'pending' mean in line 18?

7 What is referred to in the phrase 'This latter decision' (line 22)?

8 Why have various governments changed their minds so often about tricycles?

9 What is meant by 'adequate funds' in lines 23–24?

10 What does 'this' refer to in line 28?

11 What is the connection between disabled people and mass production and why does the writer suggest a different relationship could be established?

12 What does 'along these lines' mean in line 31?

13 In what ways could designers make ordinary cars suitable vehicles for disabled people, and why would they be more suitable?

14 What does 'a weekly grant' mean in line 39?

15 Why does the writer call it 'the worst of the available options' (line 40)?

[4] 46

■ In a paragraph of not more than 100 words explain the problems facing the Government with regard to transport for disabled people and how the writer thinks they could be solved.

Follow the stages outlined on pages 40–41, and in making your plan, consider whether all the six paragraphs of the original article are relevant to this question. One is not relevant at all, and two more are only marginally relevant. Above all, avoid repeating details such as those in Paragraphs 3–5.

[7] 00

■ Read the following passage carefully.

How Safe are British Dams?

At the end of January two dams in Brazil collapsed after weeks of torrential rain, leaving thousands homeless and causing millions of pounds' worth of destruction. A week earlier, a report about the American Teton dam failure, in which 11
5   people were drowned, was published. Such events raise again the question of dam safety in Britain, with the Reservoirs Act, 1975, still to be implemented. We can be sure that none of Britain's dams is completely safe. There is an accepted factor of uncertainty in any engineering project, and where nuclear
10   engineers have their 'least credible accident', dam engineers have their 1,000 or 10,000 year flood. A dam designed to stand up to a flood statistically expected only once every, say, 5,000 years, could conceivably fail a year after it was built if it experienced a 15,000 year flood.
15   Yet there is still a wide range of factors which might cause a dam to collapse, even without considering the likelihood of an event which occurs at intervals of 1,000 years or so. In Britain, the element that seems to pose the most risk is age. This problem is probably unique, or at most shared by only one or
20   two countries. According to A. I. B. Moffat of the University of Newcastle, speaking at a recent conference on the evaluation of dam safety, held in California, the average age of dams in

25 Britain is about 108 years. There are no records of the construction or subsequent behaviour of many of these and some are below present standards of safety.

Figures collated by Mr Moffat, and supported by general experience, tend to show that most dam failures occur either within the first few years of construction, or after a long uneventful period of operation. It appears that Britain's dams
30 are now approaching this stage. There is a steady upward trend of incidents which may or may not lead to a major collapse, but which call for immediate remedial action. If the trend continues, then we may expect an increasing number of such events and, sooner or later, a failure.

35 Legislation can never be perfect, and the relatively good safety record of British dams, which no doubt follows from sound engineering practice and administration, might also owe a little to luck and an equable climate.

Until now, failure to remedy a defective dam has rarely been
40 the cause of prosecution – and the penalties are very mild. Also, as Mr Moffat pointed out, some dams have never been inspected, despite the statutory obligation to do so. The new act places enforcement of its legislation in the hands of 66 local authorities. While it overcomes certain deficiencies in the Act it
45 replaces, splitting responsibility between so many small bodies could result in a standard of safety that varies widely throughout the country. Local authorities do not always fulfil the dictates of Parliament. So while the legislation can go a long way towards preventing the kind of disaster that occurred last
50 month in Brazil, its ultimate effectiveness lies in the hands of local government.

[7] 47

■ Answer the following questions on the passage.

1 What does 'which' refer to in line 4?
2 What is the connection between recent events in Brazil and the United States and the Reservoirs Act, 1975?
3 What is the meaning of the phrase 'least credible accident' (line 10)?
4 What factor of uncertainty is taken into account by dam engineers and how important is it?
5 Which 'event' is being referred to in line 17?
6 In what way is the situation of dams in Britain different from that in most other countries?
7 At what point is a dam most likely to collapse, according to the evidence?
8 Which 'stage' is referred to in line 30?
9 What is 'the trend' described in line 32?
10 What does 'which' refer to in line 36?
11 What are the main reasons for the good safety record of British dams?
12 What is meant by 'an equable climate' (line 38)?

13 In what way has the law regarding maintenance and inspection of dams been inadequate until now?
14 What 'penalties' are referred to in line 40?
15 What is wrong with the division of responsibilities in the new Act?

[7] 48

■ In a paragraph of not more than 100 words, explain why the writer is concerned about British dams and why he is not satisfied with the provisions made by the Reservoirs Act.

All the paragraphs in the original article are relevant to a certain extent, but you must find a way of stating the important facts in simple, general terms, rather than repeating details that cannot be included in the space available. For example, in Paragraph 2, there are two sentences that are clearly relevant, while the rest can be omitted from the answer. In the same way, in the last paragraph, the gist of what it is saying concerns two points, expressed   a) in the first two sentences,   b) in the conclusions to be derived from the other four.

[8] 00

■ Read the following passage carefully.

The Sun Sinks Slowly on the Western

Scene from *The Wild Bunch*, made in 1969.

What's happened to the western? For years the cowboys and Indians, the gunfighters and farmers, were the staples of the screen. For most of its history Hollywood has been if not dependent on, at least indebted to, the western for its continued popularity and success. Until recently it was a truism at the studios that the solution to the financial woes caused by too many flops was to make a western.

Similarly, the fortunes of television have, until lately, rested significantly upon the attraction of the west as a source of entertainment. Not only did the networks create their own westerns in series after successful series; they also bought up thousands of the longer Hollywood versions and showed them endlessly, in the mornings, in the afternoons, in prime time, and on the late shows. Most of these films and series repeated well-known stories with familiar characters, or character-types, but the American public responded to this familiarity not with contempt, but with the affection given an old, well-worn house slipper – based on the clear expectation of a satisfying and comfortable fit which supports and soothes without chafing. And the overseas audience, with a similar if not greater capacity for repetition, adopted the western for entertainment and escape purposes with an intensity which has yet to be adequately explained.

Yet in the 1970s the western suffered a serious decline. Few were made, and those few were not very good nor particularly successful.

Most of these films tried to debunk the mythical assumptions of earlier westerns, just as films like *High Noon* or *The Wild Bunch* used the western form to question itself. But unlike these earlier efforts, the films of the seventies lacked a clear vision of an alternative version of the west, one which was more 'realistic' than the mythical one. As a result, the western was no longer familiar and soothing; the old slipper seemed to have burst at the seams, destroying its form-fitting comfort and making adjustment difficult, if not impossible. Thus the loyal audience became less loyal and the film-makers understandably lost much of their interest in the genre. Westerns virtually disappeared from prime-time television, to be replaced by police and detective series.

What has caused the decline of the western? Many explanations are given: it could be argued, for example, that there is a natural cycle of popularity and surfeit, that this is the nadir of the cycle, and that the western will return as usual. This assumes a natural process that works independently of the other aspects of society. Or you could argue that the laws against mistreatment of horses have made the costs of producing westerns in America prohibitive. This assumes that the crucial factors are those of technique, rather than the interests of producers or audience. Another possibility is that the investors and/or the producers of films have decided for reasons of their own that westerns are no longer viable commercially, and so will not produce them. This implies a conspiracy theory – that we as the audience are subject to the whims of a few powerful men in the industry, and can see only what they permit us to see.

Each of these explanations is probably valid to some degree. But personally I prefer one which assumes that films are ideological productions – so that the popularity of a genre mainly depends on how well the ideology of the film fits the social experience of its audience. In other words, the crucial variable would be the relation between the symbolic structure of the story and the basic social consciousness required by the institutional demands of daily life. This kind of explanation is more satisfying, I believe, because it does not assume that the audience is simply a passive receptacle of what is put in front of it. Instead, the audience is seen as an active participant in choosing, with regard to its own needs, which types of stories it will watch and enjoy.

[8] 49

■ Answer the following questions on the passage.

1   What does 'its' refer to in line 5?
2   How did television networks follow Hollywood's lead with regard to westerns?
3   Why does the writer think westerns were like a house slipper?
4   What does 'those few' refer to in line 33?
5   What does 'debunk' mean in line 35?
6   Why are recent westerns not as successful as *High Noon* or *The Wild Bunch*?
7   What does 'one' refer to in line 41?
8   What does 'the nadir' mean in line 55?
9   What effect do the laws about horses have on westerns, and why?
10 Why does the possible action of the investors and/or producers of films (line 65) imply a conspiracy theory?
11 What is meant by 'ideological productions' (line 75)

12 What is meant by 'the crucial variable' (lines 78)?
13 What is meant by 'a passive receptacle' (line 85)?
14 What does 'it' refer to in line 88?
15 To what extent does the writer think audiences are free to choose what they enjoy seeing?

[8] 50

■ In a paragraph of not more than 100 words, give the evidence for the writer's belief that 'the western has suffered a serious decline' and explain why he thinks this has happened.

Note that the only part of the text explaining the western's success that is relevant is the part that does, in fact, attempt to do that; the references to the *extent* of this success are not relevant. Note also that the writer puts forward a number of reasons for the western's decline which are not, in fact, those which he considers to be the most important.

[11] 00

■ Read the following passage carefully.

Chemical Threat to Lake Nakuru

The life of Kenya's world-famous Lake Nakuru seems certain to be destroyed if a newly opened factory close to the shores of the lake continues to manufacture the highly toxic fungicide copper oxychloride. Ever since the factory's existence emerged into public notice at the end of last year, conservationists in Kenya have been urging the government to withdraw the manufacturing permit from the company, Copal Ltd. In spite of an independent report which severely criticised the production procedures and recommended the factory's immediate closure, Copal still has its licence. The continual lack of government action was instrumental in causing the World Wildlife Fund (Kenya) to suspend all new financial support for Kenya.

15   Lake Nakuru is one of a number of soda lakes scattered along the Great Rift Valley that skewers its way through East Africa, and its principal feature is as an occasional home for a large proportion of the three million or so pink flamingoes that move up and down
20 the valley. This, together with the rich selection of other birds, was the reason for making the lake area a national park in 1968. In 1973 the government accepted more than £170,000 from the World Wildlife Fund which was to be used to buy land around the lake
25 so as to extend the park to 50,000 acres. In return the government signed an undertaking not to allow man-made hazards to threaten the lake.

Because of its unusual chemistry as a soda lake, Nakuru depends heavily on a healthy growth of algae
30 to maintain its invertebrate, fish, and bird populations. If the algae perish then the lake will become almost totally impoverished biologically. According to a Netherlands university report just published on 'The possible toxicological implications of copper in Lake
35 Nakuru in Kenya', a level of 0.21 mg of copper per litre of lake would push the algae to the edge of destruction. The report also shows that the lake water currently contains 0.08 mg of copper per litre, the result of pesticide-containing run-off from sur-
40 rounding agricultural lands. The unavoidable spillage of copper oxychloride from the Copal factory would lift this to the lethal level within one year.

The World Wildlife Fund is anxious to stress that it is not blaming the factory for the recent departure of
45 the flamingoes from Nakuru; the copper effluent has not yet had time to exert its effect on the algae. Lake Nakuru is clearly just one of several temporary homes used by the birds. Within the past few weeks, however, the flamingoes have begun to return to the
50 lake in large numbers, and they are currently estimated at around 250,000. If the algae in the lake die the flamingoes, and the rest of the birds, will depart for ever, and, instead of going through cycles of biological abundance and paucity, the lake will remain
55 impoverished. Once copper levels have accumulated they cannot be removed.

Destruction of the lake could possibly be justified if the commercial venture were to be of great importance to Kenya: certainly, with its rapidly growing
60 population, the country desperately needs a healthy economy. But the economics of Copal's oxychloride operations make little sense. The company claims that 85 per cent of its output is destined for export. Why, then, locate the factory 400 miles from the coast so
65 that both raw materials and finished products will be making costly journeys? Copal also admit that they will be forced to use pure copper in the manufacture as there is an insufficient supply of scrap in the country. Recently, another factory making copper oxychloride
70 in Nairobi, using scrap metal, failed to secure an export order because its price was 20 per cent higher than that offered by a chemical company in a copper-producing country. The competitiveness of Copal's product on the world market is therefore in serious
75 doubt. The benefits of the Copal venture are difficult to envisage, and they vanish into insignificance when balanced against the harm that will be inevitably inflicted on Lake Nakuru and its neighbouring town. There is still time to prevent the damage from
80 becoming irreparable, but it is fast running out.

[11] 51

■ Answer the following questions on the passage.

1 Why are conservationists urging the Kenyan government to withdraw Copal's manufacturing permit?

2 What does 'its' refer to in line 16?

3 What does 'this' refer to in line 20?

4 Why is the government's attitude inconsistent with the terms of its agreement with the World Wildlife Fund?

5 What has been the result of this?

6 Why are the algae in Lake Nakuru important to birds like flamingoes?

7 What does 'the edge of destruction' mean in lines 36–7?

8 Why is the level of copper in the lake water as high as 0.08 mg per litre?

9 What does 'the lethal level' mean in line 42?

10 What is the reason for the flamingoes leaving Lake Nakuru?

11 What does 'they' refer to in line 56?

12 In what circumstances would the writer consider that the destruction of the lake might be justified?

13 What reasons are given for the Copal operations being unjustified?

14 What does 'that' refer to in line 72?

15 What does 'it' refer to in line 80?

[11] 52

■ In a paragraph of not more than 100 words, explain why the writer thinks that Copal's licence to operate close to Lake Nakuru should be withdrawn.

Do not include references to anything that is not relevant to this question, and where you take details into account, use the facts available in general terms.

[12] 00

■ Read the following passage carefully.

Price of Living in the High Alps

The building crane, which has become the most striking feature of the urban landscape in Switzerland, is beginning to alter the mountain landscape as well. Districts of the Swiss Alps, which up to now have consisted of only a few disconnected small communities content with selling cheese and milk, perhaps a little lumber and seed potatoes, are
5 today becoming parts of planned, developing regions. The new highway, the new ski-lift, the new multi-nationally-owned hotel will diversify the economy and raise the standard of living in the mountain areas, or so many Swiss regional planners and government officials hope.

The mountainous area of Switzerland, which accounts for nearly two-thirds of the
10 total area of the country and only 12 per cent of the total population, has always been the problem area. According to the last census in 1970, 750,000 people lived in the Swiss mountains. Compared with the rest of the country, incomes are lower, services are fewer, employment opportunities are more limited and populations are decreasing. In fact, in only one respect do mountain districts come out ahead. They have more farmers, which
15 many people do not consider to be an advantage. Seventeen per cent of the Swiss mountain population works in primary occupations, in contrast to only 8 per cent of the total population of the country.

The mountain farmers are a special breed of men. They work at least twelve hours a day in topographical and weather conditions which kill most crops and which only a few
20 animals will tolerate. About half of them work at some other job as well, leaving their wives and children to do the bulk of the farm work. In the Rhone Valley in the canton of Valais in south-western Switzerland nearly four-fifths of the farmers commute daily from their mountain farms to the large factories in the valley. In other parts of Switzerland this pattern of life is not as common, but almost everywhere non-farm
25 wintertime employment is the rule.

48

With all the difficulties inherent in working in the Swiss mountains, why should anyone resist any extension of the mountain economy? The answer, as Andreas Werthemann, editor of the Swiss mountain agriculture magazine *Alpwirtschaftliche Monatsblätter* states, is that 'when tourism becomes too massive, farming disappears'. And
30 basically there are three reasons why Switzerland needs its mountain farmers: they contribute to the food supply, they preserve the landscape, and they represent the Switzerland of nostalgia and holiday dreams.

In a country where nearly one-quarter of the land is unproductive and which produces only 45 per cent of its own food requirements, all types of agricultural enterprises must
35 be encouraged. Mountain farms, and mountain cattle, including cows, represent one-third of the total Swiss cattle population. In addition, more than one half the sheep, most of the goats and one-fifth of the pigs of Switzerland live in the mountain area.

The neat Swiss landscape of well-tended pastures and woodlands could not be maintained without mountain farmers. Their animals fertilize the pastures, and the
40 farmers care for the woods, buildings and land. Beyond the physical landscape, however, lies the whole picture of the Swiss mountains, of which farmers are very much a part: the alpine horn, the cow bells, the decorated milk pails, the shepherds' costumes, the parade of the animals up and down the mountains.

But in the real world, and especially in highly industrialized Switzerland where
45 mountain farmers are aware of the 'benefits' of city living, is it possible to maintain mountain agriculture and still solve the problems of mountain communities? The Swiss government has come to the conclusion that other kinds of employment in addition to farming must be emphasised. Yet whether it is possible to create other jobs that will not completely destroy agriculture is unknown.

[12] 53

■ Answer the following questions on the passage.

1   What is the connection between 'the building crane' (line 1) and the mountain districts of the Swiss Alps?
2   What does 'so' mean in line 7?
3   What does 'come out ahead' mean in line 14?
4   What are the main differences between the mountain regions of Switzerland and the rest?
5   What does 'which' refer to in line 19?
6   Where do the majority of farmers in the Rhone Valley work and how do they reach their work?
7   What does 'the rule' mean in the phrase 'non-farm wintertime employment is the rule' in line 25?
8   Find phrases justifying the three main reasons given for Switzerland's need for mountain farmers.
9   What does 'which' refer to in line 33?
10 The greatest proportion of which group of animals lives in the mountain areas: cattle, sheep, goats or pigs? Which group is least represented in percentage terms?
11 How do farmers contribute to the mountain landscape?
12 And how do they help tourism?
13 What does 'very much a part' mean in line 41?
14 Why is 'benefits' in line 45 written in inverted commas (' ')?
15 In what way does the attitude of the Swiss government towards the farms differ from that of the magazine editor, Andreas Werthemann?

[12] 54

■ In a paragraph of not more than 100 words, explain why mountain farmers are necessary to Switzerland and why their existence is threatened.

Do not include references to anything that is not relevant to this question, and where you take details into account, use the facts available in general terms.

[15] 00

■ Read the following passage carefully.

Liberty v Equality

Over the past century those on the left in British politics who have struggled for greater equality have never felt that this objective was incompatible with personal liberty; indeed, the assumption has always been that the two aims were complementary. For British reformers equality has always meant
5   equality of treatment, of respect for the individual, equality in the sense of an equal chance to develop one's personality and to live a full and free life. For this reason it has never been thought likely that to increase an under-privileged person's chance of a comfortable house, an adequate education, a good job or a satisfactory pension could do anything except increase his
10 freedom to have a satisfactory existence.
    But this equality of treatment is induced by the intervention of the State, either by central or by local government action, which can involve some loss of liberty. This may happen if activities leading to inequality have to be prohibited or penalized, but it can also occur if people are dealt with in broad
15 categories, irrespective of the merits of particular cases. In either situation the application of laws designed to produce greater equality can inhibit liberty.
    One example is in education. There is a powerful argument that the segregation of children according to merit after the Second World War into secondary modern schools, secondary schools, grammar schools, direct
20 grant schools and public schools militated against equality of treatment for the children, both during their education and in subsequent life. At school some had overcrowded classes, poor facilities and a constant turnover among their

25 teachers, while others got stability and careful, almost personal, tuition. Moreover, the whole effect was to produce different types of accent and patterns of behaviour which did much to reinforce the class divisions in British society, divisions which clearly make equality of opportunity, and equality of respect from officials and those supposed to serve the public, much harder to obtain.

30 It would be argued with great force that equality would be served if the system which did, and still does, exist in the small towns of the Scottish highlands and borders could be spread over the whole country. These were areas with no private schools, where the existing town school had a long tradition and a reputation for good work; and everyone – from the well-off farmer, the clergyman and the doctor, down to the unskilled labourer – sent

35 their children to the same school.

However, now that there are a large number of comprehensive schools in the same area in many cities, would liberty not be enhanced if the maximum parental choice was allowed, provided this did not have an adverse effect on the school system? When parents have two or three schools within reach,

40 and given that these schools all have room to take pupils from outside their immediate area, and if one has a reputation for athletics, another for a more permissive style of education, while a third is known to have a good music department, why not let parents choose the school they want their children to attend? This question of the school environment is accepted as being of vital

45 importance in moulding the behaviour and outlook of the young. To permit segregation according to ability is held to be damaging, as is segregation on class lines, and for this reason the kind of freedom of choice that would produce these results is prohibited to parents. Yet many local authorities go on to assume and assert that it follows that almost all freedom of choice

50 should be prohibited.

[15] 55

■ Answer the following questions on the passage.

1 What has been the attitude of reformers towards the relationship between equality and personal liberty?

2 What is the meaning of 'under-privileged' in lines 7–8?

3 What does 'this' refer to in line 13?

4 In what ways can laws designed to produce greater equality inhibit liberty?

5 What does 'a constant turnover among their teachers' in lines 22–3 mean?

6 What does 'the whole effect' (line 24) refer to?

7 How is 'equality of respect from officials (line 27) likely to be affected by the educational system in the country?

8 What is the argument against segregating children in different kinds of school?

9 How would equality be satisfactorily served if the system in the Scottish highlands and borders became universal?

10 What does 'within reach' mean in line 39?

11 What does 'their immediate area' mean in lines 40–1?

12 What is meant by 'a more permissive style of education' in lines 41–2?

13 Why are parents not allowed to choose the school they would like their children to go to?

14 What does 'it follows' mean in line 49?

15 What mistake is being made by local authorities, in the writer's opinion?

[15] 56

■ In a paragraph of not more than 100 words, explain how the application of laws designed to produce greater equality can inhibit liberty in the field of education, and what alternative proposals the writer puts forward.

In this summary, you must not only be careful not to include anything unless it is relevant to the question, but you should also avoid the temptation to allow your own views to enter the summary, whether you sympathise with the writer's point of view or disagree with it.

[16] 00

■ Read the following passage carefully.

Middlesex

Churchyard at Pinner, showing, on the right, the obelisk put up by J.C. Loudon.

Officially Middlesex should no longer exist. It lost a large proportion of its inhabitants and a good chunk of its land to the county of London under the Local Government Act of 1888, and the remains were
5 swallowed up 75 years later to satisfy the insatiable appetite, and to meet the administrative convenience, of the Greater London Council. But a bureaucratic death sentence has not so far succeeded in exterminating the individual
10 character of the area, which is suburban rather than urban, and very different from the city which in many ways has been dependent upon it – first for food and water, then for manufactured goods, and now, as always, for people.
15 Today people are Middlesex's most obvious characteristic. The county is London's densest dormitory. There is no obvious break between the houses and streets of London and the inner ring
20 where Middlesex begins – but the people who live in these places will still tell you that they live in Middlesex. The rows of semi-detached and terraced houses in which they live, and which have spread from the arterial roads and the underground railways almost to the limits of the
25 county's borders with Essex, Hertfordshire and Bucks, are undeniably monotonous, though perhaps they seem more so from the train or to the passing motorist than they do to those who live inside them. But they provide reasonable comfort,
30 patches of land on which to grow grass, flowers and vegetables, and an element of privacy.

To those who previously lacked them the acquisition of such advantages must have seemed akin to gaining a smallholding in paradise.

35 Suburbia, for all its unattractions and
disadvantages, meets the needs, albeit
inadequately, of many of those who have to work in
or near the centre of London. Critics who note the
ugliness and uniformity of the suburbs, and
40 conclude that life within them must be equally drab
and standardized, are wrong. Architects may
certainly be condemned for lack of inspiration in
designing them, in Middlesex as elsewhere, and
local authorities can be criticized, perhaps
45 particularly in Middlesex, for insisting that small
suburban areas be renamed and integrated to form
part of larger groups instead of preserving their
individuality, originality and eccentricity.
  But there is romance in the suburbs, and it shows
50 in small ways – such as the decoration of houses
and the design of gardens, in the custom of naming
houses Ivanhoe or The Poplars rather than
numbering , and in the abandonment of the city
word 'street' in favour of 'avenue', 'way' or 'close' –
55 as well as in some grander gestures of personality.
As a boy living near Pinner I used to enjoy visiting
that attractive little town, where I would sneak into
the churchyard to gaze at the tomb put up by J. C.
Loudon, the Victorian horticulturist who is credited
60 with the spreading of plane trees in so many
London squares. He erected an extraordinary
obelisk, from which two ends of sarcophagi stick
out at either side 10 feet above the ground, in
memory of his parents.
65   I would not want to end this personal memoir of
Middlesex with what might seem too close to a
lament for things past. We can regret, particularly
when we see rare glimpses of old rural Middlesex,
and the loss of some of the finest agricultural land in
70 England, but in contemplating the county as it is
today we should also recognize that, given the
economic conditions of the 19th and 20th centuries,
the development of the county for more and more
people to live in was inevitable. Perhaps it was also
75 inevitable, given the nature of the people, most of
whom want houses and gardens of their own and
are prepared to travel considerable distances from
their work to get them, that development should
have been along the lines it was.
80   Above all, I believe it should be recognized that
Middlesex is an entity worth preserving. It is more
than a name, more than a postal address and a
highly successful cricket team, and to assume that it
is London is to misunderstand the history and
85 nature of both the city and the county and to do
justice to neither.

[16] 57

■ Answer the following questions on the passage.

1 Why should Middlesex no longer exist, and
what evidence is there that it still does?
2 What do you suppose the Greater London
Council had an 'insatiable appetite' for
(lines 5–6)?
3 What do you understand by 'a bureaucratic
death sentence.' (line 8)?
4 In what way does London depend on
Middlesex for people?
5 What is the meaning of 'densest dormitory'
(lines 16–7)?
6 What does 'so' refer to in line 27?
7 What were the advantages so eagerly sought
by those who made their homes in Middlesex?
8 Why are the critics of suburbia mistaken, in
the writer's opinion?
9 In what way are local authorities in Middlesex
more to blame than in other counties, in the
writer's opinion?
10 In what way do the inhabitants of Middlesex
show themselves to be romantic in naming
houses and streets?

11 What example does the writer give of a 'grand
gesture of personality' and why was it 'grand'?
12 How did the nature of the people living in
Middlesex influence its development?
13 What does 'along the lines' mean in line 79?
14 Why is it a mistake to assume that Middlesex
is part of London?
15 What does 'neither' refer to in line 86?

[16] 58

■ In a paragraph of not more than 100 words,
summarise the writer's impression of Middlesex.

This summary is rather different from those that
have gone before in that it does not depend on
answering a specific question and eliminating
irrelevant paragraphs and sentences, but on
recognising the overall impression the writer is
trying to create – why, for example, he feels the need
to defend Middlesex and why he feels justified in
doing so. It is more essential than ever, nevertheless,
to avoid details and summarise in general terms the
content of what the writer is saying.

[19] 00

■ Read the following passage carefully.

Walking

You are walking along a narrow corridor or pavement when you observe that someone is approaching from the opposite direction. Your paths converge and at the critical moment you
5 swerve to one side to let him pass. Unfortunately he guesses wrong, and simultaneously moves the same way. You both halt to avoid a collision, exchange apologetic smiles, but then simultaneously take a step in the opposite direction and so reach a second
10 impasse. Sometimes further bobbing and weaving in unison ensues, and the situation begins to resemble a well-rehearsed dance routine. But the most striking feature of such encounters is how rarely they occur and how good we are at rescuing ourselves
15 whenever they do.

The fact is that we are extremely good at walking, which is just as well because we spend a large portion of our lives doing it. That we also seem to be aware of its importance as a skill can be gauged from
20 the inordinate significance which both parents and interested observers attach to a baby's first steps: with the possible exception of talking, no other developmental landmark is so eagerly awaited. Very recently, social psychologists have started to analyse
25 walking as a skilled performance and to catalogue the non-verbal cues which prevent mayhem breaking out on a crowded pavement. The fundamental problem is navigational: how do we manage to avoid collisions, without the aid of the
30 motorist's horns, indicators and an elaborate code of hand-signals? As we survey the oncoming pedestrian traffic, we must first decide how it is organised. Who is walking together and who alone? Convention dictates that the solitary walker must
35 acknowledge the unity of an approaching group by walking round it: to do otherwise is considered rude or even provocative. If the group is too big to permit this, it usually breaks up into smaller units to allow the lone walker to pass it without breaking the rules.
40 People who are walking together demonstrate the fact in a number of ways. They may be holding hands or talking to each other, but the most reliable sign of togetherness is deliberately maintained proximity. This is most obvious when an obstacle is

45 encountered or a corner turned: by adjusting their pace to re-establish contact with others, pedestrians make it clear that they are walking together and not merely along the same pavement at the same speed.

The latter – 'accidental' walking together – is a
50 source of embarrassment. It may be construed as spying or a clumsy attempt at a pick-up, so we go out of our way to avoid it, altering our pace or even crossing the road rather than risk having our behaviour misinterpreted. On the surface, the action
55 of walking alone along a street seems very private. But when we discover we have made a mistake – we have taken the wrong turn or walked past our destination – we tend to react as if everyone was watching us. We either try to disguise our error by
60 stopping to gaze into a shop-window whose contents are of no interest to us, or acknowledge it with an ostentatious silly-me gesture. Such reactions suggest that walkers feel on display, a view which cannot be justified by the lack of curiosity which
65 pedestrians objectively show each other.

Social psychologists at Oxford have also addressed themselves to the question of how people manage to avoid collisions on pedestrian crossings. They filmed four hours' activity on one such
70 crossing, and coded the body movements made by individuals at the moment when they passed someone coming the other way. It appears that men and women adopt quite different strategies to avoid collisions: men tend to face the person they are
75 passing while women turn their backs on them, regardless of their own age and the age and sex of the other person.

In the next few years we must expect to hear a lot more about walking from psychologists and
80 sociologists. It will sound so complicated a skill that many of us will hesitate to set foot outside our front doors for fear of violating the rules they will have revealed. But this won't deter the estimated five million Britons who treat walking, with varying
85 degrees of seriousness, as a recreation. They at least will not forget what Nancy Sinatra's boots were made for.

[19] 59

■ Answer the following questions on the passage.

1 What does 'at the critical moment' mean in line 4?
2 What is 'a second impasse' in lines 9–10?
3 Why does the situation begin 'to resemble a well-rehearsed dance routine' in lines 11–12?
4 What evidence is there that we think walking is very important?
5 What is meant by a 'development landmark' in line 23?
6 What is meant by 'deliberately maintained proximity' (lines 43–4)?
7 What does 'This' refer to in line 44?
8 How do people indicate to others that they are walking together?

9 Why is 'accidental' walking together embarrassing and what do we do about it?
10 What does 'on the surface' mean in line 54?
11 What is a 'silly-me gesture' in line 62?
12 What does 'on display' mean in line 63?
13 What did the Oxford social psychologists discover about the behaviour of men and women on crossings?
14 Who are 'They' in line 85?
15 What were Nancy Sinatra's boots made for (lines 86–7)?

[19] 60

■ In a paragraph of not more than 100 words, briefly describe the conventions people adopt when walking along pavements and crossing the street.

[20] 00

■ Read the following passage carefully.

Showing the Flag

How do you react to a flag-seller in the street? Do you hurry past on the other side? Do you buy a flag simply to avoid embarrassment? Or are you among the minority of willing buyers? Whichever category you fall into, the
5 attitudes and enthusiasms which marked the birth of the British flag-day have changed radically over the years.

The flag-day had its beginnings in 1912 and grew rapidly during the First World War, when £15 million was raised by this method. Today, perhaps in response
10 to adverse public criticism about being bombarded on all sides by too many charities, the Metropolitan Police try to limit flag-days in Greater London to four major combined onslaughts each year. Local authorities are permitted six weeks in any year for such work. Generally
15 they give preference to local causes. Charity still begins at home. Many charities, such as the Princess Elizabeth Day Committee, combine their Greater London flag-day appeals with those of other children's societies.

It was Queen Alexandra, anxious to help London
20 hospitals, who introduced Britain to the concept of selling emblems in support of charity. She got the idea from a Danish priest who sold roses from his garden in aid of local orphans. Queen Alexandra decided to sell artificial roses in the streets every June and the first Alexandra
25 Rose Day was on June 26, 1912.

The roses were made by crippled and blind girls of John Groom's Crippleage. Under the instruction of Miss Christine May Beeman, they produced 10 million pink linen roses, each with a capital 'A' stamped on a petal to

30 discourage imitators. Then 15,000 society ladies went into the streets of London in white muslin and organdie, wearing Gainsborough hats and carrying baskets of roses supported on red and cream sashes. On that first day £18,326 was collected. John Groom's Association for the
35 Disabled (as it is now called) still supplies linen roses, for which it receives nearly £10,000 each year.

The first day on which flags were sold was in August 1914. Mrs George, wife of a Monmouthshire engine driver, had the novel idea of selling flags in aid of the
40 Prince of Wales's National Relief Fund for the dependants of soldiers and sailors. The flags were to be of red and white and blue ribbon, stitched to matchsticks. She wrote to Sir Arthur Pearson, joint Secretary of the fund, to discover whether she needed special authority to sell
45 them. Sir Arthur assured her that there was nothing illegal about her enterprise, which was held in Pontypool and raised £10.

Many flag emblems of the First World War period were made from paper, cardboard or silk. Silk flags were
50 expected to produce a more lavish contribution. The flags were originally fastened with pins but increasing shortages of metal made new methods necessary; for instance, a paper emblem with a slit to fasten over a button. Today, further economies have encouraged the
55 development of adhesive emblems, which cost 50 per cent less to produce than the pinned variety, don't require so much storage space and dispense with hand assembly.

60 The rapid growth of flower and flag days gave rise to new regulations concerning street collections from 1915 onwards. The Metropolitan Police regulations quickly established 16 as the minimum age for collectors – perhaps reflecting a protest by the Headmistresses' Association in a letter to *The Times* about the exploita-
65 tion of children on flag-days. Permits to collect were granted to societies rather than to individuals. Animals were banned from accompanying collectors because they were said to cause obstruction, a regulation that may well have frustrated Nell, the champion Sheffield
70 collie, who collected £60 for the Belgians.

Today, half a century on, alternative forms of sponsorship and fund-raising schemes are increasingly being sought. Oxfam, for example, sells direct to the public from shops stocked with home-produced and recycled
75 goods. Ironically, a small batch of charity emblems was recently given to Oxfam, and items which originally cost only a few pence were offered for sale as collectors' items . . . still in the cause of charity.

[20] 61

■ Answer the following questions on the passage.

1 How do the majority of people react to flag-sellers in the street, according to the writer?
2 Why do the Metropolitan Police limit flag-days in Greater London nowadays?
3 Who are 'they' in line 15?
4 What does the phrase 'Charity begins at home' (lines 15–16) mean and why is it relevant here?
5 Why did Queen Alexandra use roses instead of flags for her first collection?
6 What is meant by 'society ladies' in line 30?
7 What does 'which' refer to in line 36?
8 What 'enterprise' is referred to in line 46?
9 Why were silk flags expected to produce a more lavish contribution?
10 What were the main reasons for changes in the design of flags over the years?

11 What is meant by 'the pinned variety' in line 56?
12 Why were new regulations concerning street collections introduced after 1915, and what were they?
13 What was the objection to children being employed as collectors?
14 How does Oxfam's way of collecting money for charity differ from traditional methods?
15 Why is it ironic that Oxfam recently received a batch of charity emblems?

[20] 62

■ In a paragraph of not more than 100 words describe how flag days began in Britain and briefly explain what changes have taken place in such collections over the past 60 or 70 years.

[23] 00

■ Read the following passage carefully.

Greenwich Newly Observed

Greenwich to most people who have been there means the Royal Naval College, the Maritime Museum, park and old observatory buildings on the hill, and the Cutty Sark, her
5 hull forever landlocked in its dock of Greater London Council concrete. Those are the attractions that drew nearly two million visitors in 1974, and will probably, in this European Architectural Heritage Year, draw
10 more than that number. For the Department of the Environment has nominated Greenwich as a special national showpiece, and we can expect architects and conservationists from all over Europe to start arriving soon by the
15 carload.

Not before time, either. For at least 15 years people have been saying that Greenwich was about to 'come up', that its blighted, benighted air of shabbiness and decay would
20 give place to a new era of residential popularity and commercial prosperity. All would be smart as paint again, as in the early years of Victoria's reign when real ladies and gentlemen lived in the houses by the park, and
25 London's first passenger railway brought the town within easy commuting distance of the City of London. Greenwich was about to enter its second golden age, people confidently predicted. It's been a long time happening.
30 The Victorian Georgian streets of West Greenwich have, it is true, achieved a new popularity with young professionals disillusioned with, or outpriced by, Islington and Hampstead. And the influx of tourists has
35 brought about a great burgeoning of the antique and restaurant trades. The borough planning committee dealt with no fewer than seven applications for change of use to restaurant in Greenwich during 1974 alone.
40 But though it implies a new prosperity this trend is not necessarily welcome to local residents or conservationists. They fear the 'boutique syndrome' of King's Road, Chelsea, where it has become increasingly difficult to

45 buy household necessities like milk or nails because tourist-oriented trading pushes out these less profitable staple items. Already in Greenwich an old established ironmonger's and tool shop has gone over to selling gaudy
50 and gimmicky tourist souvenirs. Others are likely to follow.

The cumulative effect of a steady programme of unspectacular repairs and improvements should not be understated, but
55 they must be seen against the big disappointment of 1975: failure to achieve any solution to the town centre's traffic problem. As long as a stream of cars and heavy lorries continue to thunder and rumble round the
60 market block, cutting it off from the riverside on one side and the park on the other, attempts to revive the historic town centre will always be prejudiced. Thus, though the Department of the Environment and
65 Greenwich council are giving the college estates, who own the splendid Georgian frontages on to Nelson Road, 80 per cent of the £10,000 needed to repaint their façades in white, cream and gold, experience suggests
70 that they will be looking dirty and decrepit again within one year, from diesel fumes and dust or mud thrown up by the traffic.

One project which will (with luck) be complete for the main 1975 tourist season, and
75 for which everyone is willing to applaud the GLC, is the modernisation of Greenwich Pier, on which that council is spending £93,000. No longer will visitors wait in the rain for river boats back to London, or struggle to
80 disentangle the rival merits and locations of Westminster boats, Tower boats, Charing Cross boats and hydrofoils or hovercraft. They will be able to wait under cover and, it is claimed, find their way unerringly to the right
85 gangway with the help of a single comprehensive destination board near the pier entrance. This pleases Greenwich, and it also pleases Mr Herbert Snowball, who for more

than five years has striven against both Board
90 of Trade and Kremlin red tape to bring Russian
hydrofoils to the Thames. Mr Snowball
reckons to provide a 10-minute peak-hour
frequency on the Greenwich–Tower–
Westminster run.
95   A 10-minute journey to London at 10-minute

intervals is better than the railway, opened in
1840, has ever given. That and an end to
heavy traffic in the centre could arguably do
more to conserve Greenwich than any amount
100 of smart paint, brass knockers and gilded
weather-vanes. They could make it accessible
without strangulation by traffic.

[23] 63

■ Answer the following questions on the passage.

1   Why is the 'Cutty Sark', a ship, now
    landlocked?
2   What is the writer referring to when he
    remarks 'Not before time, either' (line 16)?
3   What is the suggestion made by the phrase
    'real ladies and gentlemen' (lines 23–24)?
4   What does 'within easy commuting distance of
    the City of London' (lines 26–27) mean?
5   What does 'It' refer to in line 29?
6   Why did many young professional people
    move to Greenwich from Islington and
    Hampstead?
7   Why are residents not pleased by the new
    prosperity of Greenwich?
8   What is 'the boutique syndrome' (line 43)?
9   What are 'staple items' (line 47)?

10 What is being referred to in the phrase 'Others
    are likely to follow' (lines 50–51)?
11 Why does the writer suggest that the money
    spent on the Georgian frontages on to Nelson
    Road is being wasted?
12 What does 'under cover' mean in line 83?
13 What does 'red tape' mean in line 90?
14 What does 'That' refer to in line 97?
15 How much is 'any amount of' in (lines 99–
    100)?

[23] 64

■ In a paragraph of not more than 100 words, explain
why the writer thinks Greenwich may become more
prosperous and what stands in the way of
improvements.

[24] 00

■ Read the following passage carefully.

An Unromantic Artist

Everything we know about Constable the man indicates to us that he was remote from the *sturm und drang* which possessed the soul of a man like Benjamin Robert Haydon. Constable's diary-letters, written to his beloved
5 wife Maria, are a far cry from the ambitious agonizings to be found in Haydon's Journal. The anecdote that best defines the gulf which divided Constable from some of the most interesting of his contemporaries is the well-known story about the landscapist's encounter with
10 William Blake. 'Why, this is not drawing but inspiration!' Blake exclaimed, looking at one of Constable's sketches. 'I meant it for drawing!' his fellow-artist retorted.

This confrontation is worth a second look. What appeals to so many people today about Constable's
15 work is a certain emotional innocence. His is not a scientific analysis of natural phenomena, in the manner of the Impressionists, but a response which comes straight from the heart. Constable feels no need to add anything to the scene which is before him – merely to record it is
20 enough. Yet there is an important rider which must be added to this judgement. There are, in fact, two Constables, not one. The Constable of the finished paintings, sent to public exhibitions, is different from the Constable of the sketches which were left in the studio.
25 We are so accustomed to encountering this division among nineteenth-century artists, particularly those of the English school, that we have come to take it for granted, as one of the common-places of art criticism. The work the artist did for himself is invariably better
30 than the work he showed to the contemporary public. The difference, we assume, reflects that between the public and the private self which troubled the whole of the Romantic age. It also, perhaps, reflects the greater sophistication of the practising artist, who finds himself
35 opposed to the complacency and banality of bourgeois taste, but is still forced to make his living by pandering to it. There are certainly phrases which support this interpretation to be found in Constable's letters.

The fact remains, nevertheless, that Constable did
40 struggle to please the public, did compromise all too often his first inspiration in the finished work. The place where the vigour of his brushwork found the most spontaneous response was Paris, not London. The greatest triumph Constable ever knew occurred when a
45 group of his paintings were taken to France and exhibited there by the dealer Arrowsmith. Curiously enough, though Constable was aware of this success and gratified by the financial return it brought him, it does not seem to have interested him greatly otherwise. He was inclined to
50 be sarcastic about the praise which was lavished upon him by French artists and critics, and he never made the journey across the Channel.

Everything we know about Constable's personal character suggests that he was both thoroughly insular
55 and thoroughly anti-Bohemian. Like so many English artists before him, what he wanted most of all was to provide financial security for his family and to enjoy a modest eminence in his own community. Though he was for some time on the brink of achieving these aims, he
60 never quite pulled them off. He was always pursued by financial anxiety, though not to the extent that it plagued Benjamin Robert Haydon, who was driven to suicide by debt as much as failure. And Constable was never universally accepted by the connoisseurs of his time. It is
65 therefore ironic that he is now the most universally loved and least controversial of English artists.

[24] 65

■ Answer the following questions on the passage.

1   What does 'a far cry from' mean in line 5?
2   In what way was Constable very different from Haydon?
3   How was he different from most of his contemporaries in his attitude to art?
4   What is referred to in the phrase 'This confrontation' (line 13)?
5   What does the writer mean by saying 'There are, in fact, two Constables, not one' (lines 21–2)?
6   What does 'it' refer to in line 27?
7   What does 'that' refer to in line 31?
8   What was the problem that faced most Romantic artists?
9   What does the phrase 'all too often' (lines 40–1) tell us about the writer's opinion of Constable's attitude to the public?
10 How did Constable respond to the popularity of his painting in France?
11 What does 'it' refer to in line 48?
12 What evidence is given for the statement that Constable was 'thoroughly insular and thoroughly anti-Bohemian' (lines 54–5)?
13 What does 'on the brink' mean in line 59?
14 What does 'pulled them off' refer to in line 60?
15 Why is it ironic that Constable is now the most universally loved of British artists?

[24] 66

■ In a paragraph of not more than 100 words, describe Constable's attitude to his art.

Section 3: Structural conversion

[1] 67
Comparison

For general revision exercises on comparative forms, see Section 1, Exercise 2. The exercises that follow deal only with alternative forms commonly found in the structural conversion section of the Use of English paper.

A Compare these sentences:

She's	kinder more intelligent		than	her	brother.		
Her brother is **not**	as so	kind intelligent		as	she	is.	

■ Now change the sentences from one construction to the other.

1 My brother Alex is older than I am.
2 I am not as tall as he is.
3 I haven't got such an aggressive personality as he has.
4 He has a more violent temper than I have.
5 He is better at mathematics than I am.
6 I haven't as many friends as he has.
7 He works harder than I do.
   I don't _____.
8 His ideas are not as straightforward as mine.
   My ideas are _____.

B Compare these sentences:

*His attitude to life **is not the same as** it was before.*
*His attitude to life **is different from** what it was before.*

■ Now change the sentences from one construction to the other.

1 The hotel seems different from what it used to be.
2 The entrance is not the same as it was before.
3 In what way is it not the same as you expected?
4 It just gives me a different impression from the one I had last year.
5 The situation now is different from what it was five years ago.
   Five years ago, the situation was not _____.

6 At university, you won't meet the same sort of people as the ones you are used to in the village. The people you meet at university will be _____.

C Compare these sentences:

*He works in an engineering firm, **like** me/his father.*
*He works in an engineering firm, **as** I do/his father does.*

■ Now change the sentences from one construction to the other.

1 You should have booked your tickets in advance, like me.
2 They're going to Brighton for their holidays, as we are.
3 They all had a good time at the party, as you did.
4 I study hard, like him.
5 I wish I could go away on holiday whenever I felt like it, like her.
   I wish I could go away on holiday whenever I felt like it, as _____.
6 He plays football for England, as his father did.
   He plays football for England, like _____.

D Compare these sentences:

*He **was not only** irritable **but also** unpleasant.*
***Apart from being** irritable, **he was** unpleasant.*

■ Change the sentences from one construction to the other.

1 Apart from keeping everyone up at night with his noisy parties, he wakes us up the next morning by playing the piano.
2 He not only plays to win but also insults his opponents.
3 I've not only written to him but also tried to contact him by phone on several occasions.
4 Apart from spending all his own money, he borrows it from his sister.
5 Apart from finding the scheme expensive, I find it unattractive.
   I not only _____.
6 They not only made a complaint but also threatened to call the police.
   Apart from _____.

E Compare these sentences:

*As I get **older**, I become **more irritable**.*
***The older** I get the **more irritable** I become.*

■ In this exercise, change the sentences from the first construction to the second, using the aid given in brackets where necessary.

1 As the game went on, the players became more exhausted. (longer)
2 As I go on thinking about the situation, I feel more despondent. (more)
3 As time goes on, the situation is bound to become clearer. (longer)
4 If you go on eating so much, you will get fatter. (more)
5 If you always drive too fast, you are likely to have an accident.
   The _____.
6 If a child is well brought up, he will behave well.
   The _____.

F Compare these sentences:

*He's **the rudest** man I've **ever** met.*
*I've **never** met **such a rude** man.*

■ Now change the sentences from one construction to the other.

1 It's the best film I've ever seen.
2 I've never had to do such a difficult job.
3 I've never experienced such bad service.
4 It's the most beautiful country I've ever visited.
5 It's the most enjoyable holiday I've ever had.
   I've _____.
6 I've never read such an interesting book.
   It's _____.

[1] 68

Exclamations

Compare these sentences:

***What a** pleasant **surprise** to meet you here!*
*It's **such a** pleasant **surprise** to meet you here!*
***What nonsense** he talks!*
*He talks **such nonsense**!*
***How nice** to see you again!*
*It's **so nice** to see you again!*

■ Now change the sentences from a construction using **What** or **How** to one using **so** or **such**, and vice versa.

1 We had such a wonderful time at the party!
2 What a beautiful present!
3 He's so rude!
4 He's such a rude man!
5 What an awful mess they made!
6 How calm she was in the middle of that crowd!
7 We've had such a tiring journey!
   What _____!
8 How lucky I was to see you there!
   I _____!

[1] 69

A *If* and *unless*

Unless generally means 'if . . . not', as in these examples.

*We'll be late **unless** the train **arrives** on time.*
*We'll be late **if** the train **doesn't arrive** on time.*

■ Change the sentences from one construction to the other.

1 If they don't pay the rent by Saturday, I'll throw them out.
2 You can't take the examination unless you pay the fee.
3 You shouldn't make accusations like that if you're not sure of the facts.
4 Unless you apologise, I'll ring my lawyer.
5 If he doesn't tell us who he is, we won't let him in.
   Unless _____.
6 I think we've lost our way, unless that's the path over there.
   I think we've lost our way, if _____.

B *Provided (that), so long as* and *as long as*

These are stronger forms of **if**. Compare these sentences:

***If** there are **no** further questions, we'll end the meeting here.*

(The speaker does not really expect any further questions.)

***Provided** there are **no** further questions, we'll end the meeting here.*
***Unless** there are **some** more questions, we'll end the meeting here.*

(The speaker is inviting further questions.)

Now compare these sentences:

You can stay up late	provided (that) so long as as long as	you don't feel	tired.
	unless	you feel	

- Change the sentences from one construction to the other, using **unless** in one case and **provided that** or an alternative in the other.

  1 So long as you're not busy, I'd like to ask you some questions.
  2 Unless you object, we'll interview the next candidate now.
  3 I'm prepared to go on with the project, as long as you agree.
  4 We should have a good time, unless we get bad weather.
  5 Provided you let me know in advance, I can make the arrangements.
   I won't be able to make the arrangements _____.
  6 Unless I hear otherwise from you, we'll meet on Saturday.
   We'll meet on Saturday, so long_____.

[2] 70
Dress

Compare these sentences:

She **was wearing**	green.
She **was dressed**	in green.

She **was wearing**	a green coat.
She **had**	a green coat **on**.

- Change the sentences to the other construction shown in the same box.

  1 He was wearing black for the funeral
  2 He was wearing a black tie for the funeral.
  3 The bride was wearing a white dress.
  4 She also had a white veil on.
  5 The bridesmaids wore blue.
   The bridesmaids were _____.
  6 The bride's mother wore a diamond necklace.
   The bride's mother had _____.

[2] 71
Gerund and *it* . . . + infinitive

Compare these sentences:

> **Remembering** grammatical rules **is** sometimes **difficult**.
> **It is** sometimes **difficult to remember** grammatical rules.

The gerund form is preferred at the beginning of the sentence. The infinitive is essential when we begin the sentence with an impersonal subject, **It**, except with one or two phrases, e.g. **It is worth**, **It is no use**, etc.

- Change the sentences from one construction to the other.

  1 It is dangerous to walk on railway lines.
  2 Staying indoors all the time is unhealthy.
  3 It is a pleasant form of relaxation to play tennis at the weekend.
  4 Working for people who don't appreciate your efforts is a depressing experience.
  5 It is more expensive to live in a hotel than to live in a flat.
  6 Expecting other people to do what you would not do yourself is illogical.
  7 Marrying for love is better than marrying for money.
   It _____
  8 Meeting interesting people is always a pleasure.
   It _____

[2] 72
There is/are and *Have (got)*

Compare these sentences:

> **There is** nothing **for her** to do all day.
> **She has** nothing to do all day.
> **There are** a lot of people working under him.
> **He has** a lot of people working under him.

- Change the sentences from one construction to the other.

  1 There was no one for him to talk to.
  2 She has plenty of assistants to help her.
  3 She hasn't had any letters today.
  4 There are several patients in my ward.
  5 There should be other children for her to play with.
  6 He always has long queues of people waiting to see him.
  7 We won't have anywhere to stay.
   There _____.
  8 They have no reason to complain.
   There _____.

[2] 73

It and co-ordinate relative clauses

Compare these sentences:

> *He blamed me for his mistakes, **which was unfair.***
> *It was unfair of him to blame me for his mistakes.*

■ Change the sentences from one construction to the other.

1 It was unkind of her to take the child's toys away from him.
2 He made a fuss about nothing, which was stupid.
3 He solved the puzzle in five minutes, which was clever of him.
4 He rings me up in the middle of the night, which is extremely annoying.
5 It was foolish of them not to take your advice.
   They _____.
6 They didn't invite her to dinner, which was hurtful.
   It _____.

[3] 74

Present Perfect and Past tenses: *for*, *since* and *ago*

A   Compare these sentences:

> *The last time I saw her **was** in 1978.*
> *I **haven't seen** her **since** 1978.*
> *He **last came** here **at** the end of June.*
> *He **hasn't come** here **since** the end of June.*

■ Change the sentences from a construction using the Past Simple tense to one using the Present Perfect tense with **since**, and vice versa.

1 I last played tennis in December.
2 The last time they won the election was in 1974.
3 I haven't voted in an election since 1970.
4 He hasn't made a speech on television since Christmas.
5 The last time she travelled by air was in March.
   She hasn't _____.
6 We haven't heard from them since 1st August.
   We last _____.

B   Compare these sentences:

> *The last time I saw her **was** seven years **ago**.*
> *I **haven't seen** her **for** seven years.*
> *He **last came** here six months **ago**.*
> *He **hasn't come** here **for** six months.*

■ Change the sentences from one construction to the other.

1 I last played tennis nine months ago.
2 The last time they won the election was eleven years ago.
3 He hasn't paid the rent for five weeks.
4 I haven't heard from her for some time.
5 They haven't made a profit for ages.
   The last _____.
6 He has not been to see his mother for ages.
   He last _____.

C   Compare these sentences:

> *I **haven't seen** her **for** seven years.*
> *It's seven years **since** I **last saw** her.*

■ Change the sentences from one construction to the other.

1 I haven't played tennis for several months.
2 It's eleven years since they last won the election.
3 It's a long time since they wrote to us.
4 I haven't worked as hard as this for a long time.
5 He's been away from school for six weeks.
   It's _____.
6 It's many years since we last met.
   We haven't _____.

[3] 75

It's/It was the first time . . .

Compare these sentences:

> *I've **never seen** anything like this **before.***
> *It's **the first time** I've **ever seen** anything like this.*
> *I **had never seen** anything like that **before.***
> *It was **the first time** I **had ever seen** anything like that.*

■ Note the changes that take place in form and in tenses and then change the sentences from one construction to the correct alternative.

1 I've never spoken to him before.
2 It's the first time I've ever flown.
3 He was worried, because she had never been late before.
4 We were surprised, because it was the first time they had ever invited us to lunch.
5 He said 'no' very brusquely, although it was the first time I had ever asked him for money.
   He said 'no' very brusquely, although I had

   _____.
6 You've never made a complaint about it before.
   It's the first time _____.

[3] 76

Clauses of concession

A *although*, *though* and *even though*

Compare these sentences:

Although Though Even though	*he played brilliantly,*	*he still lost the match.*
In spite of Despite	*(his) playing brilliantly,*	

Even though is a stronger form of **although**.
In spite of and **despite** are followed by a noun or a gerund.
The clauses in these examples can be in reverse order, so that in all cases the sentences can begin: **He still lost the match . . .**
Though can appear at the end of a sentence, but not **although** or **even though**.
In balanced sentences, where the two clauses are equally important, we normally use **while**.

> **While** *there is much to be said in favour of the plan, there are also some points that must be raised against it.*

- Rewrite the sentences, using the word or words given in brackets.

  1 Although food production is rising, there are still too many people who are hungry. (In spite of)
  2 In spite of notices being put up everywhere, people still spoil the park with their litter. (Even though)
  3 They weren't able to get into the cinema, despite having queued for an hour. (though)
  4 We went on playing, although it was raining. (despite)
  5 In spite of the increase in production, we have not made a profit.
     Although we have _____.
  6 They hope the students will continue to pay, even though they have raised the fees.
     They hope the students will continue to pay, despite _____.

B *Whatever, whoever, however, wherever*

Compare these sentences:

> I don't care ⎱ *what she says. I don't believe her.*
> It doesn't matter ⎰
> *I don't believe her,* **whatever** *she says.*

> I don't care ⎱ *who he is or* **what** *his business is.*
> It doesn't matter ⎰ *He's not coming in.*

He's not coming in, **whoever** *he is and* **whatever** *his business is.*

> I don't care ⎱ **how urgent** *it is. I'm not going to*
> It doesn't matter ⎰ *stay here all night to finish it.*

I'm not going to stay here all night to finish it, **however urgent** *it is.*

> I don't care ⎱ **where** *they are. We'll find them.*
> It doesn't matter ⎰

We'll find them, **wherever** *they are.*

> I don't care ⎱ **how much** *it costs. I'm going to buy*
> It doesn't matter ⎰ *it.*

I'm going to buy it, **however much** *it costs.*

- Rewrite the sentences, using **whatever**, **whoever**, etc.

  1 I don't care who he is or where he studied. I'm not going to employ him.
  2 I don't care how polite she is. I don't trust her.
  3 It doesn't matter what you tell her or how often you tell her. She never listens.
  4 I don't care how much you paid for it. I don't want it in the house.
  5 I don't care who he is. I'm going to speak to him.
     I'm going to speak to him, _____.
  6 It doesn't matter where he has gone. He'll come back.
     Wherever he _____.

[3] 77

Because and *because of*

Compare these sentences:

> *They were unable to play* **because** *it* **was raining**.
> *They were unable to play* **because of the rain**.

- Change the sentences below from a construction using a verb to one using a noun, and vice versa.

  1 The lawyer came to see him because of his complaint.
  2 The first performance of the play was postponed because of the leading actor's illness.
  3 He deserves his success because he has worked hard.
  4 They refused to fly because it was foggy.
  5 They have made him redundant because he is old.
     They have made him redundant because of
     _____
  6 They have asked for more money because the cost of living has risen.
     Because of the _____

[3] 78

Impersonal construction: *It is said*, etc.

Compare these sentences, noting the difference between them, depending on whether the action is future, present, or past.

> **It is expected that** the President **will arrive** tomorrow.
> The President **is expected to arrive** tomorrow.
> **It's said that** the robbers **are hiding** in this area.
> The robbers **are said to be hiding** in this area.
> **It's believed that** the murder **occurred** at three o'clock.
> The murder **is believed to have occurred** at three o'clock.

■ Change the sentences from an impersonal construction (with **it**) to a personal one, and vice versa.

1 It is thought that the pilot lost his way in the fog.
2 The Prime Minister is expected to mention the subject in the House of Commons this afternoon.
3 It is reported that she is planning to resign – in the year 2000!
4 It is understood that a foreign team is negotiating his transfer for £2 million.
5 It is believed that they have discovered the cause of his illness.
  They are _____.
6 She is said to know everyone worth knowing around here.
  It's said _____.

[4] 79

The reason for/why

Compare these sentences:

> **The reason for the boy's bad behaviour** (or **The reason for the boy's [boy] behaving badly**) at school is that he is unhappy at home.
> **The reason why the boy behaves badly** at school is that he is unhappy at home.

■ Change the constructions from **the reason for** (+ a noun, if you know one, or gerund) to **the reason why** (+ a clause, with subject and verb), and vice versa.

1 The reason why food is short at present is quite clear.
2 Can you give me any reason for your absence yesterday?
3 The reason why the Government decided to stop providing tricycles for disabled people was that they were unsafe.

4 Is there any reason why taxes are being increased?
5 The reasons for my resignation are private.
  The reasons why _____.
6 I'm afraid I can't offer any logical reason why your son failed the examination.
  I'm afraid I can't offer any logical reason for

  _____.

[4] 80

May and *might*

Compare these sentences:

Perhaps he Maybe he	'll come tomorrow. knows the answer.
It's just possible that he	's working in the garden. hasn't heard the phone.
He **may**	**come** tomorrow. **know** the answer.
He **might**	**be working** in the garden. **not have heard** the phone.

■ Change the constructions used in the sentences to forms with **may** or **might**.

1 Perhaps she hasn't received our letter.
2 Perhaps his train is late.
3 It's just possible that he won't be able to come tomorrow.
4 Perhaps he didn't realise how important it was.
5 Perhaps they've got tired and have gone home.
6 It's just possible that she's waiting for you to ring her.
7 Perhaps they didn't understand the instructions.
  They may _____.
8 It's just possible that he isn't aware that we are looking for him.
  He might _____.

[4] 81

Inversion: *So* and *Not only*

You may have noticed the verb form when sentences begin with these phrases and the phrases control the verb. Inversion is almost always rhetorical and not to be imitated in your own compositions, but it seems to be the favourite structural conversion item employed by examiners.

Compare these sentences:

So quickly has the change *taken place* that few people
have noticed it.
The change *has taken place so quickly* that few people
have noticed it.
Not only would the new car *benefit* disabled people but *it*
would also benefit the motor industry.
The new car *would not only* benefit disabled people *but
also* the motor industry.

■ Change the sentences from the form using inversion
to the normal word order, and vice versa.

1 So fond are Cambridge of this structure that they
   put it in every examination.
2 So distressed was he by the news of her
   resignation that he had to take the rest of the
   week off.
3 Not only did she manage to upset most of her
   colleagues, she also had a row with her boss.
4 So strongly did she feel about the matter that she
   never spoke to him again.
5 He not only left the hotel without paying but he
   also took the television set from his room.
   Not only _____.
6 The tide came in so rapidly that they were in
   danger of being cut off.
   So _____.

[4] PT I

Structural conversion – Progress test 1

■ Finish each of the following sentences in such a way
that it means exactly the same as the sentence
printed before it.

1 Surely you haven't broken them all!
   You can't _____.
2 One of my cousins is spending the weekend
   with us.
   A cousin _____.
3 Your idea is more sensible than his.
   His _____.
4 Although it was raining, they went on playing.
   In spite _____.
5 She is considered to be the outstanding painter
   of her generation.
   She is regarded _____.
6 He'll probably arrive late.
   He's likely _____.
7 It doesn't matter what she says. He'll never
   forgive her.
   He'll never forgive her, _____.

8 He was not only intelligent, but also very
   handsome.
   Apart from _____.
9 He's the most unpleasant man I've ever met.
   I've never met _____.
10 She came in and immediately went into the
    kitchen.
    As soon _____.
11 As I get older, I become more irritable.
    The _____.
12 It's easy to amuse the children.
    The children _____.
13 You're very kind to say such things.
    It's very kind _____.
14 If he doesn't pay the rent by Saturday, he'll
    have to go.
    Unless _____.
15 They have long been accustomed to such
    disasters.
    They have been accustomed _____.
16 He wasn't able to play because he was injured.
    Because of _____.
17 She was wearing a blue dress.
    She had _____.
18 Famous singers, like Placido Domingo and
    Montserrat Caballé, have sung here.
    Such _____.
19 Perhaps he did not realise what we had to do at
    first.
    He may _____.
20 He has not been here since the end of June.
    He last _____.

[5] 82

Active and Passive forms

Those of you studying this book in conjunction with
Book 1 of the course should do the exercise on page 28
before attempting these conversions, which are
intended to test your control of the more difficult forms.
Compare the sentences below:

A crowd of 50,000 people ***are watching*** *the match.*
(The match)
The match ***is being watched*** *by a crowd of 50,000 people.*

■ Change the sentences from an active to a passive
form. An agent is not necessary unless indicated.

1 The Government are going to give
   handicapped people a new form of car.
   (Handicapped people)
2 We are considering her application for the job.
   (Her application)

3   You can pay for the tickets by cheque or in cash. (The tickets)

4   You should not post your application form later than 10th August. (Your application form)

5   No one will ever forget the contribution he made. (The contribution)

6   They did not send him a copy of the contract. (A copy)

7   They did not send him a copy of the contract. (He)

8   You will have to fill in this form before you can obtain a reduction in income tax. (This form . . . a reduction)

9   We cannot reasonably grant your request unless you provide us with more information. (Your request . . . more information) (Be careful of adverb position!)

10   They were selling the family portraits to pay their debts. (The family portraits)

11   They may already have thought of further economies. (Further economies)

12   We have already paid for the goods. (The goods)

13   We have already paid you for the goods. (You)

14   They must have thought highly of him, since they gave him such a good reference. (He . . . since he)

15   They must have thought highly of him, to have given him such a good reference. (He . . . to)

[6] 83

Inversion: *nor*

Compare these sentences:

The Government lost the election because they resorted to personal attacks on their opponents.
This was not *the only mistake they made,* **either**.
Nor was this *the only mistake they made.*

The first construction is much more common in modern spoken English, except where **nor** or **neither** is used in a short answer:

A   I'm not going.
B   Nor/Neither am I.

In written English, however, the alternative is more often found; note the inversion of the verb.

■ Change the construction in the sentences from one using **not . . . either** to one using **nor**.

1   Many people have questioned the validity of the statistics the newspaper has published about universities. This is not the only cause for disagreement with their conclusions, either.

2   Since *the Sun* changed hands, many people have criticised its political attitudes. This is not the only reason why they dislike it, either.

3   Personally, I don't like the sensational form of English it uses. I don't think it is easier for foreign students to understand than *The Times*, either.

4   With the players I've got, I don't think we'll beat Brazil in the World Cup. I don't think we'll beat Haiti, either, if it comes to that.

5   Football managers don't really say things like that. They don't usually use inverted forms in their sentences, either!

[6] 84

Inversion: *neither . . . nor*

Compare these sentences:

*The Queen does not play golf. Her husband **doesn't play** golf, **either**. / **Neither/Nor does** her husband. **Neither** the Queen **nor** her husband **plays** golf.*

Notice the singular form of the verb here.

*I **did not have** much opportunity to express my opinions **either** during the dinner **or** afterwards. **Neither** during the dinner **nor** afterwards **did I have** much opportunity to express my opinions.*

There is no inversion in the first example because **neither** and **nor** refer to nouns, **the Queen** and **Her husband**. There is inversion in the second example because **neither** and **nor** refer to the verb, to 'having an opportunity to express my opinions'.

■ Rewrite the sentences, beginning each sentence with **Neither**, and only inverting the verb form where this is necessary.

1   My father was not born in London, and my mother wasn't, either.

2   You will not find so many friendly people either in the big cities or in the holiday resorts.

3   Your qualifications do not make you a suitable candidate. Nor does your previous experience.

4   He did not distinguish himself either as a politician or as a lawyer.

5   I didn't find any reference to the events either in *the Guardian* or in *the Sun*.

6   *The Guardian* did not pay any attention to the events. Nor did *the Sun*.

[6] 85

Subject and verb agreement: *all* and *every*

Notice where singular and plural verbs are used in these sentences:

*He **is** a pleasant **person**. They **are** pleasant **people**.*
*Everyone **likes** him. **Everything is** arranged.*

The word **people** is always plural in English and we hardly ever use the form 'persons'.
On the other hand, **everyone (everybody)** and **everything** are always singular. We never say 'all people' or 'all persons' and we hardly ever use the form 'all things'. 'All the people' and 'all the things' are not often used, either.
Traditionally, **his** has been used with everyone, to refer to men and women together:

*Everyone who lives in the village has **his** own plot of land.*

However, recently, it has become increasingly common to use **his or her**:

*Each member of the group is responsible for arranging **his or her** own travel insurance.*

■ Change the construction in the sentences from a form using 'people' or 'things' to a form using **everyone** or **everything**.

1 All things come to an end, sooner or later.
2 The people who know him all like him.
3 All the people in the village look forward to the festival.
4 Have you bought all the things I asked you to buy?
5 At my time of life, all the people I have met and all the things I have seen have become a distant memory.

[7] 86

Indirect questions in reported speech

There are two problems in dealing with indirect questions in reported speech: a) the necessary changes that must be made in tense and in time and place expressions (see Exercise 21); b) a change in the verb form (interrogative to affirmative). Compare these sentences:

'Do you work in London?' he asked her.
He asked her if/whether she worked in London.
'Where is he hiding?' the policeman asked them.
The policeman asked them where he was hiding.

■ Change the sentences into reported speech, altering the word order and making any necessary changes to tense and to time and place expressions.

1 'Did you see John yesterday?' I asked her.
2 'Why aren't you coming to the party tomorrow?' she asked me.
3 'Will it be ready by tomorrow?' she asked them.
4 'How can you expect us to complete the job by next week when we haven't been told how to do it?' they asked her.
5 'How much longer must I wait before someone takes any notice of me?' he asked the clerk.
6 'Do you think they may have lost their way?' she asked him.
7 'Will I ever feel the same as I did a week ago?' she wondered.
8 'Can you imagine how long it took us to get here last night?' he asked her.
9 'How do you think I felt when I was told you were not going to arrive till tomorrow?' she asked him.
10 'Shouldn't we thank Betty and Steve for the lovely party they have given before we go home?' she asked him.

[7] 87

Indirect commands in reported speech

Commands and requests, using the imperative in direct speech, are introduced by **tell** and **ask** respectively.
Note the construction (infinitive) in reported speech:

*'**Please help** me!' she said to him.*
*She **asked him to help** her.*
*'**Don't worry** about it!' he said to her.*
*He **told her not to worry** about it.*

■ Change the sentences below into reported speech.

1 'Please don't tell him where I am!' she said to me.
2 'Finish the exercise you were doing yesterday!' he said to the students.
3 'Don't open your books until I tell you to!' he said to them.
4 'Please hand your papers to the examiner when you go out!' she said to the candidates.
5 'Don't shoot until I say "Shoot!"' the sergeant said to the recruits. Of course, they all fired as soon as they heard the word 'Shoot!'

[8] 88

That of, those of

Compare these sentences:

Its populaton is greater than $\begin{cases} Japan's. \\ that\ of\ Japan. \end{cases}$

Her crime stories are not as good as $\begin{cases} Simenon's. \\ those\ of\ Simenon. \end{cases}$

Its head was bigger than $\begin{cases} an\ average\ monkey's. \\ most\ monkeys'. \\ that\ of \begin{cases} an\ average\ monkey. \\ most\ monkeys. \end{cases} \end{cases}$

Its feet were bigger than $\begin{cases} an\ average\ monkey's. \\ most\ monkeys'. \\ those\ of \begin{cases} an\ average\ monkey. \\ most\ monkeys. \end{cases} \end{cases}$

■ Change these sentences from structures employing possessive forms to the alternatives using **that of** or **those of**.

1 His tastes are not so luxurious as his grandfather's.
2 The new law is not as far-reaching as the previous government's.
3 Our production is greater than the Soviet Union's.
4 The people here are rather taller than other islands'.
5 His general intelligence is higher than the average person's.
6 His essays show more imagination than most students'.

Note

The construction using **that of** or **those of** must be used when a possessive form is unacceptable:

The concert was not as good as $\begin{cases} last\ year's. \\ that\ of\ last\ year. \end{cases}$

Our $\begin{cases} law\ is \\ laws\ are \end{cases}$ more civilised than $\begin{cases} that\ of \\ those\ of \end{cases}$ the Middle Ages.

We cannot use 'one' or 'ones' in either case; in the second sentence, we cannot say '**the Middle Ages**' ' either. The possessive form for a period of time (**last year's**) is only used when the time expression is specific.

[8] 89

Not only and *both*

Compare these sentences:

Both the management **and** the staff are in favour of the changes.
Not only the management **but also** the staff are in favour of the changes.

The second form is a more emphatic way of expressing the first.

■ Change the sentences from one construction to the other.

1 His classes are full, both in the mornings and in the evenings.
2 Not only the Government but also the Opposition voted in favour of the proposal.
3 His success depends both on hard work and on good business sense.
4 He has always been a good speaker both in private gatherings and in front of large audiences.
5 The tragedy is that not only the films but also the negatives were destroyed in the fire.

[8] 90

Inversion: *Not only*

(See also Exercise 89.) Compare these sentences:

Not only Smith but also most of his family were involved in the crime.
Smith was **not only involved** in the crime but also the brains behind it.
Not only was Smith involved in the crime but **he** was also the brains behind it.

Note that in the first sentence, **not only** refers to Smith, and so no inversion is required although it begins the sentence. (See also Exercise 89.) In the other two sentences, **not only** refers to Smith's being involved; here, inversion of the verb is required if the sentence begins with **not only**.

■ In the following sentences, first decide whether **not only** refers to a person or thing (noun), or to an action (verb form) or adverbial phrase. In the first case, rewrite the sentence, using **both**, as in the previous exercise; in the second, rewrite the sentence, beginning with **not only**.

1 He fell in love with her not only because of her beauty but also because of her personality.
2 He not only wrote to the Prime Minister but also obtained an interview with him.
3 He not only speaks Spanish but also speaks Catalan.
4 He speaks not only Spanish but also Catalan.

5   He has the ability to please not only the audience but also the critics.

6   We find evidence of his preoccupation with form not only in his early work but also in his most recent novels.

[9] PT2

Structural conversion – Progress test 2

■ Finish each of the following sentences in such a way that it means exactly the same as the sentence printed before it.

1   Leave it here, and I'll mend it later.
I'll mend it later _____.

2   Offering me more money won't change my decision.
Even if you _____.

3   'Will I ever see her again?' he wondered.
He wondered _____.

4   I was finally able to convince him of its value.
I finally succeeded _____.

5   'Please don't do that again!' she said.
She asked me _____.

6   'Does anyone know the way to the station?' he asked.
He asked _____.

7   We queued up for hours, but we still didn't get in.
We still didn't get in, in spite _____.

8   They're building a new bridge across the river.
A new bridge _____.

9   She didn't know where it was, and I didn't, either.
Neither she _____.

10 It is certain that their English will improve in time.
Their English _____.

11 I expect she came by bus.
She must _____.

12 The police couldn't trace the owner of the car.
The owner of the car _____.

13 Did he give any reason for his behaviour?
Did he explain why _____.

14 There's no reason why you should come, if you don't want to.
There's no reason for _you to come_ _____.

15 It would be a good idea if you did it again.
You had _better do it again_ _____.

16 It's believed that the Prime Minister is planning to resign.
The Prime Minister is believed _____.

17 No one works harder than he does.
There _____.

18 You should do something about it, instead of sitting there grumbling.
You should do something about it, rather
_____.

19 'What were you doing last night?' the policeman asked them.
The policeman asked them what _they had been don... previou..._

20 He blamed me for his mistakes, which was unfair.
It was _____.

[9] 91

You/one

Compare these sentences:

*One can't help **one's** upbringing but **one** should avoid letting **oneself** be ruled by it for the rest of **one's** life.*

*You can't help **your** upbringing but **you** should avoid letting **yourself** be ruled by it for the rest of **your** life.*

One and **you** are both used to mean 'a person, in general terms'. **You** is more common in spoken English and is becoming more common in written English. Grammatically, what matters is that you are (one is) consistent and end(s) with the one you have (one has) started with.

■ Complete the following passage, using **one** or **you** (or **oneself/yourself**) and the correct form of the verb in brackets.

If you're English, _____(1) (tend) to be more aware of other people's accents than _____(2) (be) if _____(3) (come) from any other European country and _____(4) (be) likely to think about _____(5) own accent and wonder if _____(6) (make) a fool of _____(7) when _____(8) open _____(9) mouth in public. I once saw a TV programme where the flatmates of an upper-class girl laughed at her because she said 'one' while they said 'you'. Eventually, she said, 'It's not my fault. After all, one can't help it if _____(10) (be brought up) to say "one"' (can) _____(11)? I mean, if _____(12) parents have always told _____(13) to say "one", _____(14) (find) _____(15) saying "one" without realising it'. 'I'm sure you're right', her friend said. 'If you're born with a silver spoon in _____(16) mouth, _____(17) (be) bound to sound as if _____(18) (swallow) it!'

[10] 92

I wish/If only . . .

A Compare these sentences:

*It's a pity they **can't** come.*
*I wish/If only they **could** come.*
*It's a pity they **live** so far away.*
*I wish/If only they **didn't live** so far away.* (If they didn't live so far away we would/could see them more often.)

Note the changes in tense used after **I wish**, and the relationship to the tenses used in the conditional sentence that follows in the last example.

■ Change the sentences from the construction using **It's a pity** to that using **I wish/If only**.

1   It's such a lovely day! It's a pity we can't go to the beach.
2   It's a pity you don't earn more money.
3   It's a pity there isn't anything interesting on television this evening.
4   It's a pity that dress costs so much. I would love it!
5   It's a pity you have to work so hard and we don't have a chance to go out and enjoy ourselves.

B Compare these sentences:

*It's a pity you **weren't** there to see the show.*
*I wish you **had been** there to see the show.*
*It's a pity they **left** the party so early. It was rather dull afterwards.*
*I wish they **hadn't left** the party so early.* (If they hadn't left, the atmosphere would have been much brighter.)

Note the change in tense used after **I wish**, and the relationship to the tenses used in the conditional sentence that follows the last example.

■ Change the sentences, as in the previous exercise.

1   It's a pity they didn't invite more people.
2   It's a pity we made up our minds so quickly.
3   It's a pity I didn't take your advice.
4   It's a pity you couldn't come with me.
    (Use **could have**.)
5   It's a pity we've lost contact with them.

C Compare these sentences:

*Why **do** you always **drop** your cigarette ash on the carpet?*
*I wish you **wouldn't** always **drop** your cigarette ash on the carpet!*
*Why **don't** you **look** where you're going?*
*I wish you **would look** where you're going!*

In these examples, **I wish** is used for complaint, whereas in Exercise A, the examples suggest wishes or daydreams, and in Exercise B, regret.

■ Change the sentences to a form using **I wish**.

1   Why don't you pay attention to what I'm saying?
2   Why do you keep reminding me of my mistakes?
3   Why aren't you more careful?
4   Why do you always blame me when things go wrong?
5   Why doesn't the Government do something about unemployment?

[11] 93

Have/get something done and *need*

Compare these sentences:

*I must **get** my typewriter **repaired**.*
*My typewriter **needs repairing**.*

■ Change the sentences below from one construction to the other.

1   My hair needs cutting.
2   We must get the piano tuned.
3   We'll have to have the house redecorated.
4   These calculations need checking.
5   Your shoes need mending.
6   I must get my suit cleaned.
7   The central heating needs servicing.
8   Before he gets a good part in a film, his nose will need straightening.
9   My racket needs restringing.
10 You should get your teeth seen to.

[11] 94

Let's

Compare these sentences:

It's a splendid idea to go to the beach.
Let's go to the beach!
It would be a shame if we quarrelled.
Let's not quarrel!

■ Rewrite the sentences below, using **Let's** or **Let's not**.

1   It would be a good idea to ask him what he thinks about it.
2   Wouldn't it be wonderful to get married tomorrow?

3 It would be a shame to make up our minds too soon.
4 Shall we go to the cinema this evening?
5 It would be a shame to sell it.

[11] 95

Seldom, not often, hardly ever

A   Compare these sentences:

*He **seldom drinks** tea.*
*He **doesn't often drink** tea.*
*He **hardly ever drinks** tea.*

■ Rewrite each of the following sentences in *both* of the alternative forms given. Be careful of the word order of adverbs.

1 I have seldom seen a more beautiful landscape.
2 I don't often travel by train these days.
3 We hardly ever have the opportunity to play tennis.
4 He hardly ever came to the office after his retirement.
5 She doesn't often write to us nowadays.

B   Inversion

It is extremely rare to find sentences beginning with **seldom**, **not often** or **hardly ever** in modern English, except in political speeches and Cambridge examination papers. You will see from the example below that when this does happen, the verb which follows occurs in its inverted, interrogative form.

*I have **seldom** read a book written in such an execrable style.*
***Seldom** have I read a book written in such an execrable style.*

■ Change the sentences below into rhetorical English, as in the example given.

1 We do not often have the opportunity of welcoming such a distinguished speaker as yourself.
2 He would hardly ever encounter again in his life an atmosphere of such bucolic charm as that of his childhood memories.
3 The great writers of the past have seldom employed such pompous means of expression as this.
4 I do not often see a film which I would recommend so wholeheartedly to all my friends.
5 You will seldom come across anybody who has travelled as widely as he has.

[12] 96

Indirect speech: verbs specifying the way things are said

A large number of different verbs may be used in indirect speech to specify the way things are said and the content of what is said.

'How nice to be home again!' she said.
*She **exclaimed** that it was nice to be home again.*

A   ■ In the first exercise, study the list of verbs given, and then identify which one you would choose to introduce each of the 20 sentences in indirect speech. You should find a different verb appropriate in each case.

accuse, admit, advise, apologise, agree, beg, complain, deny, explain, invite, offer, order, prefer, promise, refuse, regret, remind, suggest, warn, wonder

1 'I'm going to tell you how this machine works.'
2 'Yes, I took the money.'
3 'I think your ideas are absolutely correct.'
4 'Please, please don't leave me alone.'
5 'Shoot as soon as the enemy come in sight!'
6 'If you bathe from these rocks, you may be swept out to sea, because the current is treacherous.'
7 'Will I ever become rich?'
8 'I'm not going to sign it, whatever you say.'
9 'You took the money, didn't you?'
10 'No, I didn't. I've never seen it before.'
11 'It will be in ready in time for the party, without fail.'
12 'I'd rather not go out tonight.'
13 'Remember that the Joneses are coming to dinner tonight.'
14 'Would you like me to pick you up at the station?'
15 'Would you like to spend the day with us at our beach house?'
16 'I'm sorry I spoke to you so rudely.'
17 'I wish I hadn't lost my temper.'
18 'I wish you wouldn't shout so much.'
19 'You'd better not tell Henry about it.'
20 'Why don't we all go out and enjoy ourselves?'

B   ■ In this exercise, you must decide what the speaker actually said. The same twenty verbs are used, but this time the statements are reported.

It is very important to note the constructions of the verbs in each case. For that reason alternatives are given where they are appropriate.

1 Andrew **refused to pay** the rent.
2 James **denied that he had been involved** in the crime (or **denied having been** . . .).
3 The man **promised that he would repair** the typewriter by the following Saturday (or **promised to repair** . . .)
4 The detective **accused him of robbing** the bank (or **accused him of having robbed** . . .).
5 He **wondered what would happen** to him in the end (or **wondered how, why**, etc.).
6 He **preferred not to make up** his mind immediately.
7 She **reminded him to post** the letters on his way to work (or **reminded him that he had to post** . . .).
8 He **explained the word to me** (or **explained how, why, what**, etc.).
9 She **warned** the children **not to cross** the road without looking to the right and left.
10 He **agreed that** our suggestion **was** sensible (or **agreed to** our suggestion, or **agreed with us about** our suggestion).
11 She **begged us not to tell** her father about it.
12 The officer **ordered them not to fire**.
13 He **admitted that he had made** a mistake (or **admitted having made** . . .).
14 She **invited us to have dinner** at her house (or **invited us to dinner** . . .).
15 She **offered to look after** the children while I was out.
16 He **apologised for arriving late** (or **apologised for his late arrival**).
17 She **complained that I spent** too much money on silly things.
18 He **regretted that he had not had** the chance to go to university (or **regretted not having had** . . .).
19 I **suggested that we should go out** to dinner.
20 The doctor **advised them to give up** smoking.

C ■ Now, as far as possible without checking on the constructions shown in Exercise B, rewrite all the sentences in Exercise A in reported speech, using any introductory name or personal pronoun you choose, and adding appropriate objects where necessary, e.g., **The teacher** explained **to us** . . .

[12] 97

Comparison: Emphasising differences

(See also Exercise 67.)

When we wish to emphasise the differences in a comparison between two things or people, we can do so in the following ways. Compare these sentences:

She's	much far	taller more intelligent better	*than* her brother.		
Her brother is **not nearly**			*so as*	tall good intelligent	*as* she is.

■ Change the sentences below from one construction to the other.

1 Her husband is much older than she is.
2 The hotel where we are staying is much cheaper than the one where we stayed last year.
3 He didn't do nearly as well as his sister in the exam.
4 We haven't spent nearly as much money as we did last year.
5 I found the last TV series far more interesting than this one.
6 It isn't nearly as hot as it was last week.
7 They played far better in the first match than in the final.
8 Strangely enough, I don't get nearly as much work done in the office as I do at home.

[12] PT3

Structural conversion: Progress test 3

■ Finish each of the following sentences in such a way that it means exactly the same as the sentence printed before it.

1 He doesn't like apples very much.
   He isn't very _____.
2 'Please don't tell anyone about it,' he said to me.
   He begged _____.
3 This is the procedure that all the students have to follow.
   This is the procedure that every _____.
4 'You killed her, didn't you, Jones?' said the inspector.
   The inspector accused _____.
5 My suit needs cleaning.
   I must get _____.

6   She said that she was sorry that she had not
    rung me.
    She apologised _____.
7   They all worked hard but only Sheila passed
    the examination.
    They all worked hard but Sheila was _____.
8   It's a pity I didn't think of that at the time.
    I wish _____.
9   His parents didn't let him play with other
    children.
    He _____.
10 He came in quietly because he didn't want to
    wake up his wife.
    He came in quietly so as _____.
11 Although he hasn't been working here long,
    he's already impressed the manager.
    He may not _____.
12 It's a good thing I braked. We would have
    crashed, otherwise.
    We would have crashed if _____.
13 My recovery was due to her kindness.
    It was thanks to her _____.
14 Don't touch those wires in any circumstances.
    Those wires _____.
15 In my opinion, it's the best book I've ever
    read.
    I consider it _____.
16 It would be a shame to argue about it.
    Let's _____.
17 She was sorry that she had been so rude to
    them.
    She regretted _____.
18 He prefers travelling by train to flying.
    He would _____.
19 You never know what's going to happen, do
    you?
    One _____.
20 It is difficult to reach them because of the flood
    water.
    The flood water _____.

[14] 98

Being and *as/since*

Compare these sentences:

Being an engineer,		
As	*he is* an engineer,	*he has had a great deal of experience with machines.*
Since		

Providing the subject of the second (main) clause is in
effect the same as that of the subordinate clause, the
participle can be used in this way, but note the word
order of the following:

John being out, *As/Since John was* out,	*I took the telephone call for him.*

Note the change in the position of the participle.

■ Change the sentences below from a construction
using the present participle to one using **as** or **since**,
and vice versa.

1   As he is a teacher, he has often come across
    problems like this.
2   Being so tall, you'll have no difficulty in reaching
    the top shelf.
3   Since Mary's father was so rich, she inherited a
    lot of money when he died.
4   Mary's uncle being as rich as her father, he left
    her a lot of money, too.
5   Being so rich, she has never had to worry about
    money.
6   As she was the oldest person present, she felt she
    should take the initiative.

[16] PT4

Structural conversion – Progress test 4

■ Finish each of the following sentences in such a way
that it means exactly the same as the sentence
printed before it.

1   Do you think he is like me?
    Do you think we _____?
2   'Come on, you can swim across the pool if you
    try,' he said to the child.
    He encouraged _____.
3   I agree that we could have done more to help.
    I agree that we haven't _____.
4   It is thought that a number of other people are
    involved in the affair.
    A number of other people are _____.
5   The proposal was so absurd that it was greeted
    with laughter.
    So absurd _____.
6   He raised his hand and, as he did so, knocked
    the lamp over.
    He raised his hand and, in _____.
7   'Why didn't you look where you were going?'
    he said angrily.
    He said: 'You should _____.
8   I am very interested in antiques, above all in
    silverware.
    I am very interested in antiques, but what

    _____.

9   He will not be satisfied with anything less than
the full amount.
Nothing less _____.

10   He must decide himself whether he should go
or not.
Whether he should go or not _____.

11   'Let's go, shall we?' said Fred.
Fred suggested _____.

12   She was in such a terrible state that I'll never
forget it.
I'll never forget what _____.

13   The roof collapsed as a result of the heavy rain.
The heavy rain _____.

14   I don't know how you got the idea that I'm
rich.
I don't know what _____.

15   I've never seen anything like this before.
It's _____.

16   I seldom watch that programme.
I hardly _____.

17   They had no news of his whereabouts until last
Wednesday.
It was not _____.

18   He has no cause to complain.
There's no reason why _____.

19   Jane did a lot of work during her holidays.
While _____.

20   The situation is different from what it was five
years ago.
Five years ago, the situation was _____.

[17] 99

In case and *lest*

Compare these sentences:

*I'll leave some food in the fridge for her. She **may arrive** late.*

*I'll leave some food in the fridge for her, **in case** she **arrives** late.*

*He left some food in the fridge for her **because he thought** she **might arrive** late.*

*He left some food in the fridge for her **in case** she **arrived** late.*

In case means 'because . . . may' in reference to present or future time and 'because . . . might' in reference to past time. It is followed by a verb in the Present tense when it refers to present or future, and by a verb in the Past tense when it refers to the past.

Lest is not normally found in modern English except in very formal or rhetorical contexts. It is always followed by the subjunctive (**should**).

Compare these sentences:

*I have made three copies of the will, **in case** there **is** some misunderstanding at a future date.*

*I have made three copies of the will **lest** there **should be** some misunderstanding at a future date.*

■ In all cases below, change the sentence to a construction using **in case** and a verb in the appropriate tense.

1   Take an umbrella. It may rain.

2   You'd better write this down. You may forget it.

3   He has taken out an insurance policy because he
may have an accident.

4   He took out an insurance policy because he
thought he might have an accident.

5   I have taken the precaution of informing the
Minister, lest he should think we are acting
independently.

6   You'd better offer them an alternative date.
They may not be able to come on Sunday.

7   I suggested that he should give them an
alternative date because I thought they might
not be able to come on Sunday.

8   He advised those present to consider his political
record, lest any of them should doubt the honesty
of his motives.

[18] 100

Alternatives to Conditional sentences

A   Compare these sentences:

If it hadn't been for you, we would have missed the train.
But for you, we would have missed the train.

■ Change the sentences below from one construction to the other.

1   But for his example, they would all have run
away.

2   If it hadn't been for the nurse's presence of mind,
the hospital would have been burnt down.

3   But for his prompt intervention, a fight would
have broken out.

4   If it hadn't been for his retirement, I would never
have become managing director.

5   But for their assistance, we would all have been
in trouble.

B   Compare these sentences:

*Even if you worked **as hard as possible**, you would never finish it in time.*
However hard you worked, you would never finish it in time.

Even if you had done just what he wanted, *he would not have been satisfied*.
Whatever you had done, he would not have been satisfied.

The same kind of construction is possible with **whoever** and **wherever**.

■ Change the construction in the sentences below to one employing **however**, **whatever**, **whoever** or **wherever**.

1 Even if you looked everywhere, you would never find it.
2 Even if you had offered him all the money you have, he would not have sold it to you.
3 Even if he had behaved as badly as possible, they would never have disqualified him from the tournament.
4 Even if we found a very efficient secretary for him, he would still find fault with her. (Two possibilities – with **whoever**, use 'as a secretary'.)
5 Even if you had made him the perfect proposal, he would still have turned it down.

[18] 101

Alternative form of *although* clauses

Compare these sentences:

Although he is intelligent, *he is rather immature*.
Intelligent though he is, *he is rather immature*.
Although he plays well, *I don't think he will win the championship*.
Well though he plays, *I don't think he will win the championship*.

■ Change the sentences below from one construction to the other.

1 Although the performance was excellent, I think it could have been improved.
2 Although it may appear strange, there are still plenty of people who prefer taking risks to leading a quiet life.
3 Amusing though it may have seemed to you, it was no joke as far as we were concerned.
4 Although it may be understandable, I don't think his attitude is justified.
5 Rare though this construction is in modern English, the examiners seem to be fond of it.

[19] 102

Inversion: negative adverbs

(See also Exercises 81, 83, 84, 90, 95B.)

Compare these sentences:

I could not see a good parking place anywhere.
Nowhere could I see a good parking place.
He did not realise what he wanted to do in life until after he had left university.
Not until after he had left university did he realise what he wanted to do in life.
I will not part with the painting under any circumstances.
Under no circumstances will I part with the painting.
I would never have imagined that a son of mine could behave so badly.
Never would I have imagined that a son of mine could behave so badly.

If a negative adverb is put at the beginning of a sentence, the verb form is inverted. This applies to such adverbs as: **no, neither, by no means, nowhere, at no time, never, not only**. It also applies to adverbs that have negative effect: **seldom** (= not often), **scarcely, hardly (ever), rarely, little,** etc. However, the use of negative adverbs at the beginning of sentences is a rhetorical device which sounds very strange in normal conversation and should be avoided in everyday speech and writing.
Note the inversion of the sentence below:

No one has ever spoken to me like that.
Never has anyone spoken to me like that.

■ In this exercise put each negative adverb, in italics, at the beginning of its sentence or phrase and invert the verb form.

– Ladies and Gentlemen,
It has *seldom* been my privilege to address such a distinguished company of men and women. I would go so far as to say that it is *not only* an exceptional gathering in my experience, but a gathering of so many outstanding personalities from all walks of life has *rarely* taken place and it would *hardly* be possible anywhere else in the world. In saying this, I am not flattering you. I am *not only* perfectly sincere in what I say but I will go further. We could *not* find a collection of more beautiful ladies *anywhere*. It would *not* be possible, *either*, for us to encounter a more intelligent group of people. One *rarely* has the opportunity to take part in a historic event of this nature, and I *never* imagined, when I was invited, that I would be so honoured as to be asked to make the welcoming speech . . .

– Have you ever heard such pompous rubbish?

– No, If I wanted to imitate him, I'd say: I've *never* heard such a lot of nonsense in my life.

[19] 103

Alternative to *such a . . . that*

Another rhetorical form that is disappearing from modern English is to use **so** + adj. + **a**, instead of **such a** + adj.

Compare these sentences:

*It was **such a long** journey that I felt quite tired by the time we arrived.*

*It was **so long a** journey that I felt quite tired by the time we arrived.*

■ Change the sentences below from the normal form to the rhetorical one.

1 It may seem irritating to you that you have to do such a meaningless exercise.
2 I would certainly not teach such an old-fashioned form in my classes.
3 The only reason why I have included such a misleading structure is that it is often found in examination papers.
4 I call it misleading because it cannot be substituted for the alternative in such a common expression as 'such a pity', where there is no adjective.
5 It cannot be used, either, with uncountables like 'such nonsense', which is such an appropriate expression to end the exercise with that no more needs to be said.

[20] 104

Subjunctive forms: *It's time . . .*

Compare these sentences:

*It's time **for us to go**.*
*It's time **we went** (or **we were going**).*
*He realised it was time **for him to make** a decision.*
*He realised it was time **he made** a decision.*

■ Change the sentences below from one construction to the other.

1 It's time for them to give their papers in.
2 It's time I was on my way.
3 It's time for her to take her medicine.
4 Political events made it clear that it was time for them to call an election.

5 They had done so well at the casino that they realised it was time they pocketed their winnings.
6 It's time for you to make up your mind about your future.

[20] 105

Subjunctive forms: *would rather*

Compare these sentences:

*I'd **prefer you to do** these exercises at home.*
*I'd **rather you did** these exercises at home.*
*I'd **prefer you not to invite** him to the party.*
*I'd **rather you didn't invite** him to the party.*

■ Complete the following conversations by substituting one form for the other.

1 A Do you mind if I go home early?
  B Well, there's a lot of work to be done. I'd prefer you to stay until 5 o'clock.
2 A Is he getting better?
  B I'm not sure. In any case, I'd rather you didn't mention his health when you see him.
3 A Why don't you want me to go out with him?
  B I don't think he's the right kind of boy for you. I'd prefer you not to get mixed up with him, that's all.
4 A Didn't you like my performance in the play?
  B Yes, but I'd rather you got down to some serious work.
5 A Would you mind helping me with my homework?
  B No, but I'd prefer you to show it to me after dinner.

[20] PT5

Structural conversion: Progress test 5

■ Finish each of the following sentences in such a way that it means exactly the same as the sentence printed before it.

1 He had never met such hospitable people anywhere.
  Nowhere _____.
2 If I know what you need in advance, I can arrange everything.
  Provided you _____
3 That he had been responsible for the crime was clear to everyone.
  It _____

4   I don't know any of her friends except Sarah.
    Sarah _____.

5   She insured her life, lest she should have an
    accident.
    She insured her life, in case _____.

6   I will never consent to the marriage under any
    circumstances.
    Under no circumstances _____.

7   I'm in no hurry. It's Herbert who's pressing
    for a decision.
    I'm in no hurry. Herbert _____.

8   Although he worked hard, he could not finish
    the job.
    Despite _____.

9   If she feels worse during the night, give her
    these tablets.
    Should _____.

10 If the painting were to prove valuable, it would
    be a pity to have given it away.
    Were _____.

11 Whenever she visited Farley, she remembered
    the happy times she had spent there.
    She never visited Farley _____.

12 What I like about him most is his honesty.
    His honesty, more _____.

13 Even if you'd played better, you'd still have
    lost.
    You'd still have lost, however _____.

14 I haven't heard from Susan recently.
    Susan _____.

15 They surrendered only when there was no
    hope of victory.
    Only when _____.

16 They must have thought of him as an
    important man to have treated him so well.
    He must _____.

17 I'd prefer you to sign the cheque now.
    I'd rather _____.

18 All that prevented me from hitting him was my
    respect for you.
    But for _____.

19 As a speaker, he is brilliant, but he really
    doesn't know much about the subject.
    Brilliant _____.

20 I realised I had left my keys behind as soon as I
    shut the door.
    No sooner _____.

[21] 106

Structural conversion: Revision 1

There are no further exercises in the book comparing
structures. For each of the last four units, there is an
exercise revising the main structures you have learnt in
the previous units of the course.

■ Finish each of the following sentences in such a way
that it means exactly the same as the sentence
printed before it.

1   I expect the plane was late in taking off from
    London.
    The plane must _____.

2   He prefers playing tennis to studying.
    He would _____.

3   'Don't work so hard,' I said to him.
    I suggested _____.

4   She was sorry that she had not applied for the
    job.
    She regretted not _____.

5   I have seldom seen a more interesting film.
    I have hardly _____.

6   He has long been considered the greatest living
    novelist.
    He has been considered _____.

7   'You must allow me to pay for the lunch,' I
    said.
    I insisted _____.

8   'Where were you at 11 o'clock last night?' the
    policeman asked him.
    The policeman asked him _____.

9   I haven't seen her since the end of May.
    I last _____.

10 It's a good thing you didn't tell her. Otherwise,
    she would have been upset.
    She would have been upset if _____.

[22] 107

Structural conversion: Revision 2

■ Finish each of the following sentences in such a way
that it means exactly the same as the sentence
printed before it.

1   There's no reason why they should complain.
    They have no reason _____.

2   Are you going to do any work during your
    holidays?
    Are you going to do any work while you _____?

3   How marvellous the weather has been since we
    arrived!
    What _____!

4   They looked for the manager everywhere, but
    they couldn't find him.
    They looked for the manager everywhere, but
    he _____.

5   It's unlikely that they will argue about it.
    They _____.

6   I didn't see him, and Joan didn't, either.
    Neither Joan _____.

7 Being a father himself, William could understand the parents' concern.
Since _____

8 Did they give any reason for the late arrival of the flight?
Did they explain why _____

9 You made the right decision when you resigned.
You were right _____

10 I think they should make a law against it.
I think there _____.

[23] 108

Structural Conversion: Revision 3

■ Finish each of the following sentences in such a way that it means exactly the same as the sentence printed before it.

1 You never know what's best for your children these days, do you?
One _____

2 It wasn't easy for us to get a flight because of the long waiting list.
The long waiting list made _____

3 It would be a good idea if we went through this exercise again.
We had _____

4 The piano needs tuning.
We'll have to get _____

5 They didn't let me stay up late when I was young.
I _____

6 He put his keys on a key-ring to avoid losing them.
He put his keys on a key-ring so as _____

7 Only the accountants know what the real situation is.
The accountants are _____

8 You ought to settle the matter once and for all.
It's time _____

9 I'd prefer her to answer the letter herself.
I'd rather _____

10 I've never played squash before.
It's _____.

[24] 109

Structural conversion – Revision 4

■ Finish each of the following sentences in such a way that it means exactly the same as the sentence printed before it.

1 The cause of his death was a heart attack.
He died as a _____.

2 The situation has changed considerably in the last three years.
The situation is not the same _____.

3 It is thought that the robbers used this car to make their escape.
The robbers are _____.

4 Nobody knows much about his plans for the future.
Little _____.

5 Although his attitude appears unusual at first sight, it is quite understandable.
Unusual _____.

6 I like all Mozart's operas, but my favourite is 'Don Giovanni'.
I like all Mozart's operas, but the one _____.

7 His speech lasted so long that everyone went to sleep.
So long _____.

8 They decided to give the money they had inherited to the poor.
It was decided that the money they had inherited _____.

9 He must decide for himself what his future career is going to be.
What his future career is going to be _____.

10 He said goodbye to them regretfully.
It was with _____.

Section 4: Rephrasing

A number of questions in the Use of English paper consist of sentences printed in the format given below, in which you are expected to rewrite the sentence using the word or phrase given:

EXAMPLE John inflated the tyres of his bicycle.
          blew
ANSWER   *John blew up the tyres of his bicycle.*

Many of them demand a knowledge of phrasal verbs, like this example, and in this section, there are exercises to help you develop your knowledge of such verbs, concentrating on one verb at a time.
Others depend on the knowledge of a phrase formed by a verb and a noun which could be substituted for a verb:

EXAMPLE His attitude surprised me.
          took
ANSWER   *His attitude took me by surprise.*

There are also exercises of this kind, and you should consult the appendix at the back of this book for reference.
Finally, a number of such questions depend on a knowledge of the structural alterations required when expressions similar in meaning are used:

EXAMPLE No one came except John.
          apart
ANSWER   *Apart from John, no one came.*

Alternatively, some questions demand the substitution of a noun form for a modifying word or adjective or adverb:

EXAMPLE John was the only one who came.
          exception
ANSWER   *With the exception of John, no one came.*

Note that in cases like this, a knowledge of the correct prepositions is vitally important.
The exercises that follow are not at first in examination format, which demands a good deal of mind-reading on your part to discover what the examiner is thinking of. They are designed, instead, to show you as many variations as possible so that you know what to look for, and gradually absorb a number of expressions as alternatives to those you know already which will be useful to you in terms of your general knowledge of English usage.

[1] 110

Phrasal verbs: *turn*

■ Rewrite the following sentences, substituting the verb **turn** in the correct tense and the correct preposition for the words printed in italics, which form an equivalent to the phrasal verb.

EXAMPLE The dog suddenly *attacked* me.
ANSWER   *The dog suddenly turned on me.*

1 I was wondering when you *would arrive*. You're late.
2 He *refused* the job because they didn't offer him enough money.
3 We thought the party would be boring, but it *proved* better than we had expected.
4 The factory *produces* 100 cars a day.
5 He could not earn enough money as a teacher so he *took up* journalism.
6 Thousands of people *made the effort to attend* the procession, in spite of the bad weather. (Use 'to see.')
7 Don't waste any more time trying to find it. It will *be found by chance* somewhere.
8 He was *evicted from* his cottage for not paying the rent.

[1] 111

Rephrasing

■ Rephrase the following sentences, using the words or phrases given, and adding whatever is necessary.

1 It's just like him to forget your address.
   It's typical _____ him _____.
2 Unlike you, I am not very interested in making money.
   The difference _____ that I am not very interested in making money.
3 I've earned just over £100 this week.
   I've earned _____ than £100 this week.
4 Provided you pay the rent by next Monday, I won't take legal action.
   I'll take legal action against you if _____.
5 Alex is very like his sister.
   Alex and his sister are very much _____.

81

6   The tickets cost less than I had expected.
    The tickets didn't cost _____ I had
    expected.
7   Their attitudes are alike.
    They have _____ attitudes.
8   He paid more for the house than it was really
    worth.
    The house was not really _____ he paid
    for it.
9   The journey was so tiring that we were all
    exhausted by the time we arrived.
    It was _____ that we were all exhausted
    by the time we arrived.
10 We have been offered the same conditions.
    The conditions you have been offered are the
    same _____ me.

[2] 112

Phrasal verbs: *make*

■ Rewrite the following sentences, substituting the
verb **make** in the correct tense and the correct
preposition for the words printed in italics.

1   He has such a strange accent that I can't
    understand what he is saying.
2   He was too ill to go to the party so we bought
    him a toy to *compensate for* his disappointment.
3   Bad service does not *contribute to* good relations
    between companies and their customers.
4   He is not as honest as he *pretends*.
5   He spends the evenings *inventing* stories for the
    children.
6   How many stamps do you need to *complete* the
    set?
7   The prisoners are believed to be *going in the
    direction of* London.
8   The sign was so far away that I couldn't
    distinguish what it said.
9   He *transferred* all his property to his son.
10 I was very upset when we quarrelled and I'm
    happy that we've *become friends again*.

[2] 113

Phrases with *make*

A number of phrases, employing **make** and a noun, can
be used instead of a verb. For example, compare the
following:

*At dawn, the enemy **attacked** us.*
*At dawn, the enemy **made an attack on** us.*

Note that there are sometimes problems in deciding
which preposition follows the noun in such cases, and
in knowing the correct noun to use.

■ Rewrite the sentences below, replacing the verb with
a phrase employing **make** and the appropriate noun,
using prepositions where necessary.

1   They have complained to the management.
2   Now you will have to choose.
3   They have offered me the job.
4   I hope you succeed in what you are doing.
5   The police have been enquiring into the
    matter.
6   I'm not going to excuse his behaviour.
7   I think you are mistaken.
8   The Minister spoke on television.
9   I'd like to use this idea, if you don't mind.
10 He travelled across the Sahara Desert.
11 Hurry up! We'll be late.
12 You shouldn't say funny things about people
    who are disabled.

[2] 114

Rephrasing

Rephrase the following sentences, using the words or
phrases given, and adding whatever is necessary.

1   She came in and switched on the light.
    The moment _____ on the light.
2   You're very kind to take so much trouble.
    It's _____ take so much trouble.
3   It's easy to keep the children under control.
    The children _____ under control.
4   We seem to be unable to make progress without
    destroying things.
    We seem to be incapable _____ without
    destroying things.
5   Do you mind having to work by yourself?
    Do you mind having to work _____ own?
6   It's no use arguing about things you can't change.
    _____ point _____ about things you
    can't change.
7   Who's responsible for the sales department?
    Who's _____ charge _____ the sales
    department?
8   He makes regular inspections of the factory.
    He makes inspections of the factory _____
    intervals.
9   I am sure I can count on your co-operation.
    I am sure I can count on _____ together.
10 I think it would be useful to consider the proposal.
    I think the proposal would be worth _____.

[3] 115

Phrasal verbs: *bring*

■ Rewrite the following sentences, substituting the verb **bring** in the correct tense and the correct preposition for the words printed in italics.

1 The meeting was nearly over when he *raised* the problem of the new salary scales.
2 It won't be easy to *convert him* to our way of thinking.
3 We hope to *publish* your book before Christmas.
4 It's the best thing that has happened in women's fashion since they *introduced* the mini-skirt.
5 His kindness gradually *caused* a change in her attitude.
6 Her parents died when she was young and she was *reared* (not 'educated') by her aunt.
7 Throw some water on her face. Perhaps that will *revive her*.
8 He was caught in the rain last night. That must have *been the cause of* his cold.

[3] 116

Rephrasing

Rephrase the following sentences, using the words or phrases given, and adding whatever is necessary.

1 He'll probably arrive late.
He's likely _____.
2 She is considered to be the greatest actress in the world.
She is regarded _____ the greatest actress in the world.
3 They have long been accustomed to problems of that kind.
They have been accustomed to problems of that kind for _____.
4 He likes apples very much.
He _____ fond _____ apples.
5 I consider what he is saying to be a lot of nonsense.
My opinion _____ a lot of nonsense.
6 All of them sent their kindest regards.
They _____ their kindest regards.
7 Many people are unaware of what has been achieved.
Many people _____ know what has been achieved.
8 The shops are easily accessible.
The shops are _____ reach.

9 At some country parks, there may be an admission fee.
At some country parks, you may _____ an admission fee.
10 However, the charge is no more than £1.
However, it only _____ £1.

[4] 117

Phrasal verbs: *come*

Rewrite the following sentences, substituting the verb **come** in the correct tense and the correct preposition for the words printed in italics.

1 I *found* this old diary *quite by chance* in my desk.
2 Look! The crocuses and all the other spring flowers have *started to bloom*.
3 Do you think this question will *arise* at the next meeting?
4 How on earth did that *happen*? It seems strange.
5 He has *received* a lot of criticism because of his policy. (two prepositions)
6 I don't know if this experiment will *succeed*, but it's worth trying.
7 We seem to have *encountered* an insoluble problem. (two prepositions)
8 I can't understand what *took possession of* you for you to behave so rudely.
9 I was very disappointed in the film, which did not *reach the level of* our expectations. (two prepositions)
10 He *inherited* a fortune when his aunt died.

[4] 118

Comparative verb structure

Verbs with similar meanings may have different structures and you could be asked to recognise the differences.

■ Rewrite the sentences below using the alternative verb given in brackets. In all cases, some change must be made in the structure.
Look at the example:
She is considered to be a great actress. (**regarded**)
She is **regarded as** *a great actress.*

1 Have you managed to solve the problem yet? (**succeeded**)
2 Did he explain why the machine broke down? (**account for**)
3 All I am asking you to do is to answer my question. (**reply**)

4   Several people have written in for the job. (**applied**)
5   Many people are not aware of what has been achieved. (**know**)
6   I can't allow you to park here. (**let**)
7   What time do you expect the plane to reach London? (**arrive**)
8   Can you tell me how it is done? (**explain**)
9   Tell me what it is like. (**describe**)
10 I didn't like it very much. (**appeal**)

[4] 119

Rephrasing

■ Rephrase the following sentences, using the words or phrases given, and adding whatever is necessary.

1   What was the cause of the delay?
    What was the reason _____ the delay?
2   Surely she didn't leave the baby alone in the house?
    She can't _____ the baby alone in the house?
3   Did he give any reasons for his behaviour?
    Did he explain _____?
4   Perhaps he didn't understand what he was supposed to do.
    He may _____ what he was supposed to do.
5   They may well have been surprised that you rang them in the middle of the night.
    They _____ probably surprised that you rang them in the middle of the night.
6   I don't think he's sufficiently well to be moved from the hospital.
    I don't think he's _____ enough _____ to be moved from the hospital.
    (Which space is unnecessary?)
7   The Government aims to provide special cars for these people.
    The Government aims to provide these people _____.
8   Handicapped drivers are going to be supplied with special cars.
    Special cars _____ handicapped drivers.
9   His stamp collection costs him a lot of money.
    He spends _____ his stamp collection.
10 He spent two hours doing the shopping.
    It took _____ the shopping.

[5] 120

Phrasal verbs: *go*

■ Rewrite the following sentences, substituting the verb **go** in the correct tense and the correct preposition for the words printed in italics.

1   As time *passed*, he got used to his new surroundings.
2   She has *suffered* a great deal in the past year.
3   Why is there such a crowd outside? What's *happening*?
4   Milk *deteriorates* very quickly in hot weather.
5   I've decided to *enter for* the Proficiency examination. (two prepositions)
6   Please *continue*. I'm sorry I interrupted you.
7   He thanked them for inviting him, and *afterwards said* how much he had enjoyed the evening. (You will need to change the construction following the phrasal verb here.)
8   There's not enough food to *cater for everyone*.
9   You should not have *broken* your promise. (two prepositions)
10 Your tie *matches* your suit *very well*. (Note word order.)
11 No one saw the thieves' faces. All we have *to be guided by* is the number of the car.
12 The Government threatened to raise taxes, but did not have the courage to *carry out* such an unpopular measure. (two prepositions)

[5] 121

Comparative verb structure

■ Rewrite the sentences below using the alternative verb given in brackets. In all cases, some change should be made in the structure.

1   We persuaded him not to resign. (**convinced**)
2   If that noise goes on, I'll go mad. (**drive**)
3   This sort of action is likely to produce trouble. (**lead**)
4   Did you have a good time at the party? (**enjoy**)
5   We eventually compelled them to give us back the money. (**made**)
6   I don't think I can afford to buy a new television. (**have**)
7   He has difficulty in making ends meet. (**finds**)
8   I have always thought of him as an honest person. (**considered**)
9   I advised him not to take any medicine without consulting the doctor. (**suggested**)
10 Would you recommend these cold cures to people? (**advise**)

[5] 122

Rephrasing

■ Rephrase the following sentences, using the words or phrases given, and adding whatever is necessary.

1   He spoke to her kindly because he didn't want to alarm her.
    He spoke to her kindly _____ to alarm her.
2   They have locked the door so that the cat will not get out.
    They have locked the door to prevent _____.
3   They built a high wall to make it impossible for the prisoners to escape.
    They built a high wall so that _____.
4   The thief wore gloves so as not to leave fingerprints.
    The thief wore gloves to avoid _____.
5   He sent them to university to give them a good education.
    He sent them to university so that _____.
6   I expect they were enjoying themselves, because they were laughing and singing.
    They must _____, because they were laughing and singing.
7   It was not until the train had left the station that I realised that I should have got out.
    I _____ that I should have got out _____ the train had left the station.
8   It seemed that they had not understood the difficulties involved.
    They _____ the difficulties involved.
9   You were not responsible for the accident.
    You were not _____ blame for the accident.
10 We have already posted the tickets to your address.
    The tickets _____ to your address.

[6] 123

Phrasal verbs: *put*

■ Rewrite the following sentences, substituting the verb **put** in the correct tense and the correct preposition for the words printed in italics.

1   I won't *tolerate* your insults any longer. (two prepositions)
2   The meeting has been *postponed* for a week because the boss is away.
3   She *made a special effort* to make everyone feel at home. (Use a reflexive form.)
4   I was lucky you were able to *give me a bed* for the night.
5   His opponent's remarks *caused him to lose concentration*, and he played badly.
6   He *saves £5* every week towards his summer holiday.
7   The air crash was *considered to be due to* engine failure. (two prepositions)
8   When I accused him, he *assumed* an innocent expression.
9   He has *offered* his house for sale.
10 Could you *connect me with* your sales office, please? (two prepositions)

[6] 124

Rephrasing

■ Rephrase the following sentences, using the words or phrases given, and adding whatever is necessary.

1   He doesn't know how much it cost, and his wife doesn't, either.
    Neither he _____ how much it cost.
2   All students are expected to register before the beginning of term.
    Every _____ to register before the beginning of term.
3   Thanks to their hard work, they succeeded.
    _____ was due to their hard work.
4   Sheila hasn't written to us recently.
    We _____ from Sheila recently.
5   They should seek legal advice, rather than take the law into their own hands.
    They should seek legal advice, instead _____ the law into their own hands.
6   Why didn't you take your medicine after breakfast? Now it's too late.
    You ought _____ your medicine after breakfast. Now it's too late.
7   Why don't you borrow the money from the bank?
    Why don't you _____ you the money?

8   He has lived here all his life.
    He has lived here since
    _____.

9   It's strange that none of the newspapers
    mentioned it.
    It's strange that none of the newspapers
    referred _____.

10 It's strange that none of the newspapers
    mentioned it.
    It's strange that it _____
    the newspapers.

[7] 125

Phrasal verbs: *stand*

■ Rewrite the following sentences, substituting the
verb **stand** in the correct tense and the correct
preposition for the words printed in italics.

1   He *took the place of* the leading actor, who was
    ill. (two prepositions)

2   The painting is so good that it *is easily
    distinguishable* from the others in the
    exhibition. (Note word order.)

3   If you are not prepared to *defend* yourself, how
    can you expect us to help you? (two
    prepositions)

4   The letters UNO *represent* the United Nations
    Organisation.

5   These components are expected to *work, in
    spite of* great pressure. (two prepositions)

6   I will *honour* the agreement.

7   Do you expect me to *look on* and do nothing
    when I see a friend being attacked?

8   I'm not prepared to *put up with* any more
    insults from you.

9   When he heard that the President had
    decided to seek re-election, he *withdrew his
    candidacy*.

10 We *are in favour of* a fair day's pay for a fair
    day's work.

[7] 126

Comparative verb structure

■ Rewrite the sentences below, using the alternative
verb given in brackets. In all cases, some change
must be made to the structure of the sentence.

1   The floods caused the dam to collapse.
    (**resulted**)

2   The collapse of the dam was caused by the
    floods. (**resulted**)

3   They were against the plan because they
    thought it would be too expensive. (**cost**).

4   The question of dam safety has once again
    arisen because of the recent accident in Brazil.
    (**raised**)

5   His warnings are the consequence of the
    research he has carried out. (**arise**)

6   I am glad to hear that he has got over his
    illness. (**recovered**)

7   It is a pity that we failed to contact him before
    he left the country. (**succeed**)

8   The Prime Minister said something about it
    in his speech. (**commented**)

9   He has replaced another actor, who was not
    available. (**substituted**)

10 I was afraid that he would start a fire in the
    house with his experiments. (**set**)

[7] 127

Rephrasing

■ Rephrase the following sentences, using the words
or phrases given, and adding whatever is necessary.

1   No one was there.
    There _____ there.

2   There have been no changes made to the
    plans since our last meeting.
    No _____ the plans since our last
    meeting.

3   No one works harder than he does.
    There _____ works harder than he does.

4   He was too busy to pay any attention to me.
    He had _____ to pay any attention to
    me.

5   He speaks too slowly to sound convincing in
    the part.
    He doesn't _____ to sound convincing
    in the part.

6   They arrived too late for us to be able to make
    use of them.
    They arrived so _____ able to make use
    of them.

7   The law has not yet been implemented.
    The law has not yet been _____ effect.

8   Most dam failures occur soon after
    construction or much later.
    Most dam failures take _____ soon after
    construction or much later.

9   Under the new law, local authorities have
    been made responsible for dams.
    Under the new law, local authorities have
    been put _____ dams.

10 Do you think we are the same height?
    Do you think she is as _____?

[8] 128

Phrasal verbs: *take*

■ Rewrite the following sentences, substituting the verb **take** in the correct tense and the correct preposition for the words printed in italics.

1 I won't *occupy* any more of your time.
2 I know you're upset at missing the train, but that's no reason to *relieve your irritation by blaming* the porter. It's not his fault. (it + two prepositions)
3 When I'm too old to play tennis, I'll *adopt* golf *as a pastime*.
4 You can see from his nose that he *resembles* his father.
5 Flight 123 to Paris will *leave the runway* in five minutes.
6 They have been buying shares in the hope of *gaining control of* the firm.
7 I'm afraid you've been *tricked*. These pearls are not genuine.
8 He *imitated* the Prime Minister perfectly on television last night.
9 The children have *developing a liking for* their new teacher.
10 I have received your report and will *raise* the matter with the department concerned.

[8] 129

Phrases with *take*

■ Rewrite the sentences below, replacing the verb with a phrase employing **take** and the appropriate noun, using prepositions where necessary.

1 I wouldn't pay any attention to them if I were you.
2 Where did the accident happen?
3 It's wonderful to hear that she has agreed to participate in the ceremony.
4 These problems must also be considered.
5 Why were you offended by what he said?
6 Look after yourself!
7 As the police refused to listen to their complaints, they decided to act as if they were the law themselves.
8 The thieves obviously profited from your absence to get into the flat.
9 He assumes that I will help him whenever he is in trouble.
10 He didn't mean to upset you. You mustn't let it affect you deeply.

[8] 130

Rephrasing

■ Rephrase the following sentences, using the words or phrases given, and adding whatever is necessary.

1 For many years, Hollywood depended on the western for much of its success.
For many years, Hollywood owed
_____.

2 Not only did the television companies buy westerns from Hollywood, but they also created their own series.
The television companies not only
_____.

3 Not many westerns were made in the 1970s, and they were not very good or very successful.
_____ westerns were made in the 1970s, and they were neither
_____.

4 Film-makers lost interest in westerns when they ceased to be profitable.
Film-makers were no _____
westerns when they ceased to be profitable.

5 The crucial factors are technical ones.
The crucial factors are
_____ technique.

6 The audience likes to be an active participant in deciding what films shoould be made.
The audience likes to take
_____ in deciding what films should be made.

7 He no longer lives in this neighbourhood.
He doesn't _____ in this neighbourhood
_____.

8 The success of a film depends not on its quality but on the reaction of the audience.
The success of a film depends on the reaction of the audience, rather
_____.

9 It would be a good idea if we left now.
We had _____ now.

10 I agree with you to a certain extent.
Up _____, I agree with you.

[9] 131

Phrasal verbs: *carry*

■ Rewrite the following sentences, substituting the verb **carry** in the correct tense and the correct preposition for the words printed in italics.

1 It is one thing to plan a new town, and another to *put* the plan *into practice*.

2 He *continued* working although he was tired.
3 He *behaves* as if he were the owner of the place.
4 He lost his place in the middle of his speech, but *brought* it *to a successful conclusion, in spite of that*, so that no one noticed. (Use 'so well that no one . . .')
5 He *brought* the project *to a successful conclusion* in spite of the problems.

[9] 132

Phrasal verbs: *think*

■ Rewrite the following sentences, substituting the verb **think** in the correct tense and the correct preposition for the words printed in italics.

1 Now that I *remember* it, aren't you the young man who gave me a lift home last Sunday?
2 We are *considering the idea of* going to Italy for our summer holidays.
3 I can't say 'Yes' or 'No' to the plan now. I must have time to *consider* it *at length*.
4 *Imagine* what would happen if the level of the water in the river rose three metres in a single night!
5 I'll *give consideration to* your proposal and let you have my decision tomorrow.

[9] 133

Rephrasing

■ Rephrase the following sentences, using the words or phrases given, and adding whatever is necessary.

1 No one helped me, except Michael.
Michael was _____ helped me.
2 Only Sarah passed the examination.
Sarah _____ passed the examination.
3 I don't know any of her acquaintances except Michael and Sarah.
Michael and Sarah _____ I know.
4 Do you still say that you will not help us?
Do you still refuse _____?
5 You have to keep your wits about you in this sort of situation, don't you?
One _____?
6 I'm not worried about the cost of the holiday. What worries me is the time it will take to get there.
I'm not worried about the cost of the holiday. It's _____ worries me.

7 He appears to know what he's talking about.
He sounds _____ what he's talking about.
8 Judging from those black clouds over there, we're likely to have some rain.
Judging from those black clouds over there, it looks as _____ rain.
9 We didn't take those photographs in Glasgow. We took them in Edinburgh.
We didn't take those photographs in Glasgow. It was _____.
10 I've never thought of that before.
That has never occurred _____ before.

[10] 134

Phrasal verbs: *look*

■ Rewrite the following sentences, substituting the verb **look** in the correct tense and the correct preposition for the words printed in italics.

1 I'm *trying to find* my pen. Have you seen it anywhere?
2 I *anticipate* meeting you again *with pleasure*. (two prepositions)
3 I'll *take care of* the children while you're out.
4 We *regard* this invention as one of the most important in modern times.
5 I must stay in tomorrow. Some people are coming to *view* the house, *to see if they want to buy it*.
6 I'll *investigate* the matter, Madam, and find out what has happened.
7 I have *respected and admired* him since I was a small boy. (two prepositions)
8 She *despises* us because she belongs to an exclusive club. (two prepositions)
9 I couldn't just stand there, *taking no active part*, when I saw him attacking the girl.
10 Don't *rely on* him for help.

[10] 135

Comparative verb structure

■ Rewrite the sentences below, using the alternative verb given in brackets. This word must *not* be altered in any way. In all cases, some change must be made to the structure of the sentence.

1 I advised him to go and see a doctor. (**suggested**)
2 It made me remember my childhood. (**reminded**)

3 I refuse to pay more for it than it is worth.
  (**object**)
4 I'd prefer to walk, if you don't mind. (**would
  rather**)
5 I wouldn't want to see that film again.
  (**couldn't face**)
6 I regret telling her about it. (**am sorry**)
7 Would you mind my bringing a friend with
  me? (**object**)
8 I felt obliged to interrupt him. (**couldn't
  help**)
9 He doesn't usually get up so early. (**is not
  used to**)
10 I couldn't bear to work for a man like that.
   (**couldn't stand**)

[10] 136

Rephrasing

■ Rephrase the following sentences, using the words
  or phrases given, and adding whatever is necessary.

1 I'm afraid the books haven't arrived yet.
  I'm afraid the books still _____.
2 He doesn't like working during the holidays.
  He doesn't like working while he _____.
3 The first performance was good, but the
  second was even better.
  The first performance was good, but the
  second was better _____.
4 We had better leave soon. Otherwise, we'll be
  late.
  If_____.
5 He prefers walking to going by car.
  He would _____.
6 It's a pity I didn't know you were in town last
  week.
  I wish _____.
7 'Why don't you go and see the doctor?' she
  said.
  She suggested _____.
8 If you need any attention during the night,
  please ring this bell.
  Should _____.
9 If you left the company now, you would find it
  very difficult to get another job.
  Were _____.
10 Why do they always put records on at this
   time of night?
   I wish _____ at this time of
   night.

[11] 137

Be + preposition

■ Substitute the verb **be** in the Present tense, together
  with the correct preposition, for the words printed in
  italics.

1 It's obvious that he *is keen to get* promotion
  from the way he speaks to the boss. (two
  prepositions)
2 I *am going* to Bangkok tomorrow.
3 We must have a chat about it as soon as the
  conference *is finished*.
4 Tonight's concert *has been cancelled* because of
  the illness of the soloist.
5 He *is not at home* at the moment. I'll let you
  know as soon as he *returns*.
6 If I *haven't gone to bed* by the time you come
  home, I'll make you some coffee. (Use '*still
  . . . when . . .*')
7 What*'s the matter*? You look upset.
8 Oh, dear, we *haven't any* butter *left*. I forgot to
  buy some. (two prepositions)
9 What *is being shown* on television tonight?
10 Those children *are* always *doing* something
   mischievous. (two prepositions)

[11] 138

Rephrasing

■ Rephrase the following sentences, using the words
  or phrases given, and adding whatever is necessary.

1 I seldom pay any attention to what he says.
  I hardly _____ any attention to what he
  says.
2 It would be a shame to throw away all the
  work we have done.
  Let's _____ throw away all the work we
  have done.
3 Your hair needs cutting.
  You should _____.
4 'He made such a fuss,' she said. 'You can't
  imagine it.'
  'You can't imagine _____
  made,' she said.
5 I don't think the mistakes that have been
  made were his fault.
  I don't think he was _____
  the mistakes that have been made.
6 I doubt if the changes will affect us much.
  I doubt if the changes will have
  _____ us.

7 Large numbers of people are heading for the coast this weekend.
This weekend people are heading for the coast _____.

8 The company's policy is not very sensible.
The company's policy does not _____.

9 Why argue when nothing can be done about it?
What is the _____ when nothing can be done about it?

10 The success of the experiment is doubtful.
It is doubtful _____.

[12] 139

Expressions with *make* and *do*

Look at these sentences:
*She's **done her best**, but she's still **made** a lot of mistakes.*
***Do** me a favour, will you, and **make an appointment** at the dentist's for me.*

As a general rule we can say that **do** tends to relate to actions, **make** to causing, creating or constructing. Here is a list of the commonest expressions, excluding phrasal verbs, for reference:

do

better	good	repairs
one's best	harm	right
business	homework	a service
damage	an injury	wonders
one's duty	a job	work
evil	justice (to)	worse
an exercise	a kindness	one's worst
a favour	an operation	wrong

make

an apppointment	faces (at)	a report (on, to)
arrangements	a fool (of)	a request
attacks (on)	friends (with)	room (for)
the best (of)	fun (of)	a search (for)
certain (of, about)	a fuss (about)	a speech
a change	a guess	a success (of)
a choice	haste	sure (of)
a complaint	a journey	a trip
a confession	a mistake	trouble (for)
a decision	money	use (of)
a demand	the most (of)	a voyage
a difference (to)	a movement	war (on)
a discovery	an offer	way (for)
an effort	peace (with)	(someone)
enquiries	preparations	welcome
an escape	a profit	work (for others)
an excuse (for)	progress	

■ Complete the exercise without looking at this list. Then check your answers against the list. Use an appropriate form of **do** or **make**.

A I see the Civil Service are _____(1) preparations to go on strike next week. The Government has _____(2) them an offer of 7% but they say it's not enough. If they are public servants they should _____(3) their duty and not _____(4) trouble for everyone else.

B I don't think you _____(5) justice to them. After all, they don't _____(6) much money, compared with people in industry. Everyone _____(7) fun of them and the newspapers have _____(8) a lot of attacks on them recently, but most of them _____(9) their jobs well. They have to be very patient when the public _____(10) complaints about them.

A If the Government closed half the offices, they would be _____(11) us all a favour. If those bureaucrats had to _____(12) business in competition with companies abroad, if they had to _____(13) a profit every year in order to _____(14) a success of their jobs, it would _____(15) a difference to them. They'd _____(16) their best, instead of _____(17) work for other people because they're too lazy to _____(18) their own jobs properly.

B I'm not _____(19) excuses for them, but you can't expect them to _____(20) more than they're paid to do. They don't _____(21) the decisions about taxes and so on. That's the Government's responsibility.

[12] 140

Rephrasing

■ Rephrase the following sentences, using the words or phrases given, and adding whatever is necessary.

1 The landscape could not be maintained without the farmers.
If there _____, the landscape could not be maintained.

2 It is not entirely clear whether the situation will remain unchanged in the future.
Whether the situation _____ is not entirely clear.

3 Whether it will be possible to create other jobs that will not destroy agriculture is not known.
No one _____ that will not destroy agriculture.

4 She works much harder than her husband.
Her husband does not
_____.

5 It is very difficult to cultivate anything in such conditions.
The conditions make _____.

6 'This is the best way of doing it,' he told us.
He explained _____ the
best way of doing it.

7 'Don't forget to ring your aunt this evening,'
my wife said.
My wife reminded _____.

8 'I'll give you a hand with the luggage,' he
said.
He offered _____ me a hand
with my luggage.

9 He said that he was sorry he had not
contacted me before.
He apologised _____
contacted me before.

10 'Be careful when you come to that crossing,
because there have been a lot of accidents
there,' he said.
He warned me _____ a lot
of accidents there.

[13] 141

Phrasal verbs: *set*

■ Rewrite the following sentences, substituting the
verb **set** in the correct tense and the correct
preposition for the words printed in italics.

1 They *started their journey towards* London early
in the morning. (two prepositions)

2 He *made an effort* to prove he was a good
workman.

3 We have *established* a branch office in
Manchester.

4 I must *make a start on* getting the dinner ready.

5 The thief broke the electric circuit and *caused
the alarm to ring*.

6 The rings were *displayed* in the jeweller's
window.

7 Every month I *save* some money for my old
age.

8 The wallpaper is bright, and *makes the carpet
more attractive because of the contrast*.

9 He was *attacked* by a gang of youths.

10 Winter seems to be *establishing itself*.

[13] 142

Rephrasing

■ Rephrase the following sentences, using the words
or phrases given, and adding whatever is necessary.

1 I felt too tired to walk any further, so I took a
taxi.
As _____, I took a taxi.

2 There's no reason why you should be upset
about it.
There's no reason for _____ be upset
about it.

3 'Take me to the manager immediately. I must
see him,' she said.
She insisted _____ the
manager immediately.

4 I urged him to act with caution in view of the
situation.
I tried to convince him _____ with
caution in view of the situation.

5 They sought the thieves throughout the
neighbourhood.
They searched the neighbourhood
_____ the thieves.

6 They didn't make as much money from the
collection as they expected.
They felt that they could _____ money
from the collection.

7 There being no further business, the meeting
broke up at 10 o'clock.
Since _____ no further business, the
meeting broke up at 10 o'clock.

8 Of course it's mine.
Of course it _____ me.

9 I hope you don't mind me saying this.
I hope you don't object _____.

10 You should provide your students with an
example.
You should set _____ your
students.

[14] 143

Phrasal verbs: *work*

■ Rewrite the following sentences, substituting the
verb **work** in the correct tense and the correct
preposition for the words printed in italics.

1 If we sell 20 machines for £100,000, that *amounts
to* £5000 each. (two prepositions)

2 We have *devised* a system for improving the
delivery of materials.

3 The play gradually *increased in excitement to reach* a
climax. (two prepositions)

4   Everything *resulted* according to plan.
5   We're still *busy with* a solution to the problem.

[14] 144

Comparative verb structure

■   Rewrite the sentences below, using the alternative verb given in brackets. This word must *not* be altered in any way. In all cases, some change must be made to the structure.

1   He made the jury believe in his innocence. (**convinced**)
2   Can't you persuade him to try again? (**convince**)
3   They have substituted plastic bottles for the old glass ones. (**replaced**)
4   Who is going to take your place while you're away? (**substitute**)
5   His uncle left him a lot of money. (**inherited**)
6   I insist on seeing the manager. (**demand**)
7   I insist on the manager coming down immediately. (**demand**)
8   He proposed to her. (**asked**)
9   I don't think you can trust computers to solve all your problems. (**rely**)
10 A mistake of this kind could cause the wrong person to be arrested. (**result**)

[14] 145

Rephrasing

■   Rephrase the following sentences, using the words or phrases given, and adding whatever is necessary.

1   Being a nurse, Mary was able to help the victims of the accident.
    As _____, Mary was able to help the victims of the accident.
2   The heavy rain caused the river to burst its banks.
    As a result _____ burst its banks.
3   Everyone else liked the play, except Herbert.
    Herbert was _____ the play.
4   As the cat jumped on the table, it scattered the cups everywhere.
    The cat jumped on the table and, in _____, scattered the cups everywhere.
5   I like all fruit, but I like apples more than anything else.
    I like all fruit, but I like apples _____ all.

6   He will not be satisfied with anything but the truth.
    Nothing _____.
7   It doesn't matter how often you tell him. He never listens.
    He never listens, _____ you tell him.
8   Whoever believes that must be out of his mind.
    Anyone _____ must be out of his mind.
9   They all deserted him, and no one would help him.
    He was deserted by all of them, without _____ him.
10 How did you get the impression that I was planning to resign?
    What _____ the impression that I was planning to resign?

[15] 146

Phrasal verbs: *give*

■   Rewrite the following sentences, substituting the verb **give** in the correct tense and the correct preposition for the words printed in italics.

1   I have *stopped* smoking several times, but I always start again.
2   My windows *overlook* the square. (two prepositions)
3   He swore he had nothing to do with the crime, but his fingerprints *betrayed him*.
4   I'm not going to *retire from the contest* as long as I have any chance of winning.
5   The food for the voyage would have *been completely used up* if they had not rationed it.
6   When I opened the bottle, it *sent out* a peculiar smell.
7   I will not *yield* to threats of violence.
8   It was *announced* that the Minister would be coming to the reception.
9   He has *resigned from* his job and retired to the country.
10 His life was *abandoned* to idle pleasures.

[15] 147

Rephrasing

■   Rephrase the following sentences, using the words or phrases given, and adding whatever is necessary.

1   He has some difficulty in maintaining his concentration.
    He finds _____ his concentration.

2   'Come on, you can get to the top if you try,' he
    said to the children.
    He encouraged _____ get to
    the top.
3   His poor eyesight added to his problems as a
    student.
    His poor eyesight made it
    _____.
4   It has never been thought that education and
    freedom could have conflicting aims.
    No one _____ that
    education and freedom could have conflicting
    aims.
5   Why not let him choose his own career?
    What is wrong _____ his own career?
6   He is accepted as being an expert on the
    subject.
    It is _____ an expert on the
    subject.
7   Segregation according to ability is thought to
    be bad, as is segregation on class lines.
    Both _____ to be bad.
8   The school has a reputation for high academic
    standards.
    The school is reputed _____ high
    academic standards.
9   The maximum choice should be allowed,
    provided this does not have an adverse effect
    on the system.
    The maximum choice should be allowed,
    unless _____ an adverse
    effect on the system.
10 It is known that he is interested in buying the
    house.
    He is _____ interested in buying the
    house.

[16] 148

Phrasal verbs: *do*

■   Rewrite the following sentences, substituting the
    verb **do** in the correct tense and the correct
    preposition for the words printed in italics.

1   It has *no relation to* my affairs. (Use *nothing . . .*)
2   It is a bad law and the Government should
    abolish it. (two prepositions)
3   The dress *fastens* at the back.
4   We are going to have the living-room *redecorated*.
5   The baker's is shut, so I'm afraid we'll have to
    eat something other than bread this evening.

[16] 149

Phrases with *do*

■   Rewrite the sentences below, replacing the verb
    with a phrase employing **do** and the appropriate
    noun, using prepositions where necessary.

1   The fire damaged the house considerably.
2   The dog won't harm you.
3   He asked too much for repairing the car.
4   I would always be happy to serve you in any
    way.
5   To be fair to him, I don't think he really meant
    to deceive you. (Begin: 'To do . . .')

[16] 150

Rephrasing

■   Rephrase the following sentences, using the words
    or phrases given, and adding whatever is necessary.

1   I was always happy to visit the old town.
    I always enjoyed _____ the old town.
2   They decided to set up a different form of
    administration.
    It was decided _____.
3   Elsewhere, the problems are quite different.
    _____ places, the problems are quite
    different.
4   They should make a law against it.
    There ought _____ a law against it.
5   In personal terms, London depends on the
    surrounding counties for much of its wealth.
    In personal terms, London owes
    _____.
6   Why didn't they consult the people before
    they put this law into effect?
    They should _____ the
    people before they put this law into effect.
7   I don't feel like listening to your complaints
    this morning.
    I'm not in the _____ your complaints
    this morning.
8   I begged him not to do anything so foolish.
    I appealed _____ anything so foolish.
9   In my view, it is worth preserving the
    building.
    In my view, the preservation
    _____.
10 The underground is very convenient for
    commuters.
    Commuters _____ very
    convenient.

[17] 151

Phrasal verbs: *call*

■ Rewrite the following sentences, substituting the verb **call** in the correct tense and the correct preposition for the words printed in italics.

1 Building a new bridge will *demand* a large sum of money.
2 She gave him back his engagement ring and *cancelled* the wedding.
3 He was willing to help but his services were not *required*.
4 He was *ordered to join the army forces* the day war broke out.
5 He *urged* them to resist oppression.

[17] 152

Phrasal verbs: *keep*

■ Rewrite the following sentences, substituting the verb **keep** in the correct tense and the correct preposition for the words printed in italics.

1 *Don't go on to* the grass!
2 They *maintained* a lively correspondence for several years.
3 You will have to *remain on good terms with* the boss if you want to make progress in this firm. (two prepositions)
4 I wish you wouldn't walk so fast. I can't *help falling behind* you. (two prepositions)
5 The department has been closed down, but the workers have been *retained*.

[17] 153

Rephrasing

Up to now, these exercises have been laid out in a form that enables you to see where the change must be made in the sentence in order to rephrase it, using the alternative words or phrases given. The format in the Proficiency examination, however, is to supply one word, as follows:

EXAMPLE   John inflated the tyres of is bicycle.
           blew
ANSWER   *John* **blew up** *the tyres of his bicycle.*

This is more difficult because it is sometimes necessary to read the examiner's mind in order to discover what he or she is thinking of. Look at this example from a previous Cambridge paper:
I appreciate all your reasons for doing that. (**quite**)

The answer is presumably:
I quite appreciate your reasons for doing that.
but it could just as well be:
I think your reasons for doing that are quite understandable.
Do not allow this warning to put you off. The only way to deal with the situation is to try to think of saying the same thing in a different way. Almost certainly, the word given will then occur naturally to you in context. While I have adopted the Cambridge format for these exercises for the final eight units, I have occasionally made notes to help you where I consider the alternative word given is not immediately recognisable in context.

■ For each of the sentences below, write a new sentence as similar as possible in meaning to the original sentence, but using the word(s) given. These must *not* be altered in any way. (You cannot change 'take' to 'took' or 'takes', for instance.)

1 I cannot do it without your help. (**unless**)
2 They have a right to demand redundancy payments. (**entitled**)
3 I hope that we can co-operate on this project. (**together**)
4 Tell me what it is like. (**describe**)
5 We cannot force them to accept it against their will. (**made**) (Note that it is not 'make'.)
6 You will have to decide, one way or another. (**choice**) (Note that it is not 'choose'.)
7 Have you applied to the university for a grant? (**application**)
8 Have you applied to the university for a grant? (**submitted**) (Note your answer to the previous question.)
9 Some critics say that Rembrandt painted it. (**attribute**)
10 The Queen cannot take the side of any political party, lest she should be defeated with it. (**in case**)

[17] 154

Sentence completion 1: use of tenses

Another form of test used in the Cambridge Proficiency examination is to ask you to complete sentences with a suitable word or phrase. In general, two or more words are required.

EXAMPLE   Even if I had stood on a chair, I _____ reach the light bulb.
ANSWER   Even if I had stood on a chair, I *wouldn't have been able to* reach the light bulb.

As in the form of test described above, students are often confused by not knowing what the examiner is thinking of. The exercises of this kind which follow have therefore been written so that the spaces left contain similar problems grouped together, such as the use of tenses, modal forms, etc. In the test papers at the end of the book, as in the examination itself, the items are mixed and no help of this kind is given, but it is hoped that by that time you will recognise what is likely to be missing.

■ Complete the sentences below with a suitable word or phrase.

1 Although I _____ the film already, I don't mind seeing it again.
2 By the time he retires at Christmas, he _____ the firm for 40 years.
3 We _____ friends since we were at school together.
4 I think he played very well, considering that he _____ for several months.
5 By the time he _____ mind what to have, everyone else was half-way through the first course.
6 When he was at school, he is said _____ an excellent student.
7 I've been abroad for seven years, so it's a long time since we _____.
8 Don't interrupt me! I _____ I'm talking about!
9 When you _____ the washing-up, will you dust the dining-room, please?
10 We'll still be working while they _____ themselves on holiday.

[18] 155

Phrasal verbs: *run*

■ Rewrite the following sentences, substituting the verb **run** in the correct tense and the correct preposition for the words printed in italics.

1 We must order some more before we *use up our supplies*.
2 I *met* your brother *by chance* in the street yesterday.
3 I'm not prepared to listen while you *criticise* my best friend.
4 Don't *assume* that the job will be easy. (Two prepositions, and use 'idea'.)
5 There's nothing seriously wrong with me. I'm just *overtired*, and in need of a rest.
6 Let's *quickly check* the main points of the article again.
7 Unfortunately, her dog was *hit by a car* and killed.
8 I'm afraid we can't *afford* such an expensive holiday.

9 My driving licence *expires* next week.
10 I've never *encountered* such an unpleasant man. (two prepositions)

[18] 156

Rephrasing

■ For each of the sentences below, write a new sentence as similar as possible in meaning to the original sentence, but using the word given. This word must *not* be altered in any way.

1 I never pass that house without thinking of Uncle James. (**Whenever**)
2 I must object to this method of questioning. (**protest**)
3 His sudden resignation has aroused speculation. (**rise**) (Note that it is not 'raised' or 'risen'.)
4 We reached the station after midnight. (**arrived**)
5 He called on the mayor as a sign of respect. (**respects**)
6 It's a long time since you called on us. (**visit**) (Note that it is not 'visited'.)
7 I very rarely see him these days. (**hardly**)
8 Has Mary written to you recently? (**heard**)
9 We've run out of sugar. (**left**)
10 The police have abandoned their search for the missing children. (**called**) (Note that there may be ingenious ways round this sort of question, but the correct phrasal verb is usually what is required.)

[18] 157

Sentence completion 2: Conditional forms, *I wish, If only . . .*

■ Complete the sentences below with a suitable word or phrase.

1 If I had known that it would make him angry, I _____ that question.
2 _____ before you go on holiday, have a good time!
3 I wish you _____ his face when he opened the present.
4 I wish they _____ such a noise every night. I can't sleep!
5 She would have passed the exam if she _____ harder.
6 Had I not lost your address, I _____ to you.

7   If only I _____ coming! I would have made a cake.
8   Should anyone _____ while I'm out, please take a message.
9   If I _____ the lottery, I would buy a new house.
10 We would be grateful if you _____ by return of post.

[19] 158

Phrasal verbs: *break*

■ Rewrite the following sentences, substituting the verb **break** in the correct tense and the correct preposition for the words printed in italics.

1   Let's *stop work* for a while and have some tea.
2   We can *separate* the process into four stages, which will make it easier to understand.
3   My car *came to a stop*, and I had to walk.
4   The war *started* without warning.
5   The meeting *ended* at 10:00, and everyone went home.
6   She *collapsed in tears* when she heard the terrible news.
7   The burglars *entered* the house *by force* and stole the television.
8   'You've no right to say that!' he *suddenly said in a violent manner*.
9   School *ends for the holidays* three days before Christmas.
10 The police *dispersed* the crowd of demonstrators.

[19] 159

Rephrasing

■ For each of the sentences below, write a new sentence as similar as possible in meaning to the original sentence, but using the word(s) given. These must *not* be altered in any way.

1   I noticed two people approaching me. (**towards**)
2   She is afraid to go out at night, for fear of being robbed. (**in case**)
3   Volunteers are being accepted in the army, regardless of their age. (**young**) (Note that it is not enough to say, 'although they are young'.)
4   The experts filmed people's behaviour on one such crossing. (**kind**)
5   We will probably hear a great deal about this in a few years' time (**likely**)

6   Walking sounds so complicated a skill when the experts discuss it. (**such**)
7   This won't deter dedicated walkers. (**put**)
8   As soon as I came in, the phone rang. (**no sooner**)
9   You advised him sensibly. (**advice**)
10 I am opposed to that suggestion. (**disagree**)

[19] 160

Sentence completion: inversion

■ Complete the sentences below with a suitable word or phrase. Many, but not all of them, contain forms which require the verb to be inverted.

1   Not until I had read the book again _____ its true meaning.
2   I had a wonderful time at the party, and _____ my wife.
3   Seldom, since I began my career, _____ the opportunity of working with such truly professional people.
4   She says Mrs Brown wasn't happy about the divorce. Neither _____ .
5   Not only _____ late, but they don't even apologise!
6   Neither the Prince _____ a bicycle.
7   Only after a great effort _____ in carrying the boxes upstairs.
8   Only the _____ if the shoes really fit her.
9   Under no circumstances _____ to your marrying that man.
10 Rarely _____ any notice of their fathers when they say things like that!

[20] 161

Phrasal verbs: *fall*

■ Rewrite the following sentences, substituting the verb **fall** in the correct tense and the correct preposition for the words printed in italics.

1   Attendance at cinemas has *decreased* in recent years.
2   We invited the President to speak, but he cannot come. It's a good thing we have another speaker to *turn to*. (two prepositions)
3   He applied for a number of jobs but they all *came to nothing*.
4   Everything *resulted* according to plan.
5   I *was strongly attracted to* her as soon as I saw her.

6   They have *failed to keep up* with the payments, so the company have reclaimed the television set.

7   I never expected them to *quarrel*. They always seemed such good friends.

8   He finally *agreed to* my suggestion. (two prepositions)

9   It's a clever plan. Do you think they will *be deceived by* it?

10   The support he had been counting on *evaporated* in the week before the election.

[20] 162

Rephrasing

■ For each of the sentences below, write a new sentence as similar as possible in meaning to the original sentence, but using the word(s) given. These must *not* be altered in any way.

1   What do you do when you see a flag-seller? (**react**)

2   She got the idea from a friend of hers. (**gave**)

3   We have changed our methods in recent years. (**changes**)

4   The flags were sold in aid of the blind. (**help**)

5   This week, there is a 50% reduction in the price of washing powder. (**half**)

6   I'd prefer you not to come home so late. (**would rather**)

7   Could you help me, please? (**mind**)

8   He went to sleep as soon as he got into bed. (**fell**)

9   On our way to Norway, we'll stop off for a few days in Amsterdam. (**break**)

10   It was the Queen who introduced flag days to Britain. (**person**)

[20] 163

Sentence completion: modals

■ Complete the sentences below with a suitable word or phrase.

1   The house is beautiful. It _____ him a lot of money.

2   I'm sorry I was so rude. I _____ to you like that.

3   It's raining. You had _____ your umbrella.

4   I'm sure I saw him in the street this morning. You _____ done. He's in Australia.

5   I'd rather you _____, instead of telling me lies.

6   I _____ French when I was ten years old.

7   If you go to the library, they _____ able to give you the information you're looking for.

8   There are plenty of reasons why he may be late. He _____ his train, for example.

9   He spoke so softly that I _____ him to repeat the question.

10   You've broken another vase! You _____ to be more careful!

[21] 164

Phrasal verbs: *get*

■ Rewrite the following sentences, substituting the verb **get** in the correct tense and the correct preposition for the words printed in italics.

1   He is very intelligent and sure to *make progress* in life.

2   We're trying to *organise* a football team to play against the next village.

3   I've *recovered from* my illness now, and feel much better.

4   He *isn't on very good terms* with the people who work with him. (Use 'very well'.)

5   This terrible weather *depresses* me.

6   I ran after the thief but unfortunately he *escaped*.

7   You said you would help me to wash up. Don't try to *avoid* it. (two prepositions)

8   He is so charming that he can insult people and *not be punished for* it. (two prepositions)

9   I know what you're *suggesting* but I'm sure that you're wrong.

10   He's *approaching* eighty (years old). (two prepositions)

[21] 165

Phrases with *get*

■ Rewrite the sentences below, replacing the verb with a phrase employing **get** and the appropriate noun, using prepositions where necessary.

1   That whining voice of his irritates me.

2   We mustn't lose control of the situation. (Use 'let'.)

3   It's about time you threw that old overcoat away.

4   He's a clever businessman. It's not easy to outwit him. (Use 'better'.)

5 He borrowed a lot of money and couldn't pay it back. (Rephrase the second half of the sentence, using 'debt'.)
6 The result of the argument was in doubt for some time, but eventually we gained the advantage. (Use 'hand'.)
7 How did you come to believe that it wasn't true? (Use 'head'.)
8 He found the job difficult at first, but he soon became accustomed to the rhythm. (Use 'stride'.)
9 He was badly beaten in the fight. (Use 'worst'.)
10 He has a bad temper, so don't provoke his anger. (Use 'side'.)

[21] 166

Rephrasing

■ For each of the sentences below, write a new sentence as similar as possible in meaning to the original sentence, but using the word given. This word must *not* be altered in any way.

1 Who lent you the money? (**borrow**)
2 Can you account for the loss of the money? (**explanation**)
3 I'll help you, on condition that you help me in return. (**provided**)
4 He owes money. (**debt**)
5 You must look after your own interests in this world. (**One**)
6 Haven't they told you all about it? (**explained**)
7 How much did it cost you? (**pay**)
8 I like it very much. (**attractive**)
9 I don't mind whether he comes or not. (**matter**)
10 There was no need for you to have done all this by yourself. (**needn't**)

[21] 167

Sentence completion 5: connectors and modifiers

1 You may have imagined we were old friends from the way we were talking, but as a _____, we first met a week ago.
2 Of course we could sell the shares, but _____ hand there is something to be said for holding on to them.

3 I'm not altogether convinced by what you say – _____ words, I think you're making a mistake.
4 We may eventually be justified in making a bid for the company, but _____ being, I think we should let things take their course.
5 There are a number of reasons I could advance in favour of the proposal. _____ place, it is obviously to our financial advantage.
6 I wish I could share your optimism about the project, but _____ truth, I don't think it will succeed.
7 I don't really agree with what you say, although I support your ideas _____ extent.
8 The performance was not perfect, but _____ whole it was a reasonable attempt at a difficult play.
9 Take the car to the garage and get some petrol, and _____ meantime, I'll go to the post office.
10 How can you possibly vote for such a man when you've told me over _____ that you can't stand him?

[22] 168

Phrases with *have*

■ Rewrite the sentences below, replacing the verb with a phrase employing **have** and the appropriate noun, using prepositions where necessary.

1 I don't object to anything you have proposed.
2 He has certainly influenced the course of events.
3 I must admit that my poor health has affected me.
4 I don't know how he could have been cruel enough to drown the kitten. (Use 'heart'.)
5 I talked to him for a long time.
6 I didn't interrupt them, because I saw they were involved in a serious conversation.
7 Their interests are quite different. (Use 'common'.)
8 I don't know how he was cheeky enough to say it.
9 You're not entitled to criticise me. (Use 'right'.)
10 Did you enjoy yourself at the party?

[22] 169

Rephrasing

■ For each of the sentences below, write a new sentence as similar as possible in meaning to the original sentence, but using the word given. This word must *not* be altered in any way.

1   It was reasonable to imagine I would find you here. (**might**)
2   He was obviously concerned about something. (**mind**)
3   I tried to dissuade him from doing anything so foolish. (**persuade**)
4   He tends to get worried about unimportant details. (**tendency**)
5   They are not really much like one another. (**alike**)
6   They share very few interests. (**common**)
7   How was I to know what you were planning? (**expect**)
8   I've known him all my life. (**born**)
9   I was about to give them up for lost, when they arrived. (**point**)
10 It would be difficult for me to ask her for money. (**hardly**)

[22] 170

Sentence completion: verb forms, other than tenses

■ Complete the sentences below with a suitable word or phrase.

1   I can't see as well as I used to. I must _____ tested.
2   He's always had to catch the 7 o'clock train to work so he _____ up early.
3   Let's go out and enjoy _____.
4   He was so funny that I couldn't help _____.
5   We searched for the children all night, but it was not until dawn _____.
6   I'm tired. It's time we _____ bed.
7   They locked the door to prevent _____ in.
8   Neither Mr Smith nor Mrs Smith _____ their daughter was. That's why they reported her disappearance to the police.
9   I wonder why _____ from John recently. Perhaps he's not well.
10 Incredible _____, the story I'm going to tell you is absolutely true.

[23] 171

Phrasal verbs: *see*

■ Rewrite the following sentences, substituting the verb **see** in the correct tense and the correct preposition for the words printed in italics.

1   Will you *deal with* this customer, please, Miss Jones?
2   *Accompany* them *to the door*, will you?
3   He pretended to be a rich businessman, but we *were not deceived by* him.
4   We're going to the airport to *wave goodbye to* them.
5   It's six o'clock. I must *make the arrangements for* the dinner.

[23] 172

Phrasal verbs: *hold*

■ Rewrite the following sentences, substituting the verb **hold** in the correct tense and the correct preposition for the words printed in italics.

1   There are two things to be discussed which were *deferred* from the last meeting.
2   The train was *delayed* because of fog.
3   Do you think the rain will *stay away* until we get home?
4   I don't *approve of* letting children do just what they like.
5   They *continued to resist* for three days before the enemy broke through their defences.
6   The Minister said he could not *offer* much hope of an early end to the strike.

[23] 173

Rephrasing

■ For each of the sentences below, write a new sentence as similar as possible in meaning to the original sentence, but using the word given. This word must *not* be altered in any way.

1   The Council has received applications from a number of candidates. (**submitted**)
2   We only need one notice-board to provide the information. (**enough**)
3   The improvements please the workers as well as the management. (**both**)
4   This is a better service than the railway has ever given. (**such**)
5   We are no more to blame than anyone else. (**little**)

6   They don't know much about the true facts. (**ignorant**)

7   Do you think you can trust him? (**confide**)

8   The Prime Minister has been told what happened. (**informed**)

9   The crowd was estimated at considerably more than a hundred thousand. (**over**)

10 It took the jury a long time to reach a verdict. (**arrive**)

[23] 174

Sentence completion: introductory verbs in reported speech

■ Complete the sentences below with a suitable word or phrase, but avoid using forms of 'say' or 'tell'.

1   She _____ dealt with my request earlier, and said she would handle it straight away.

2   The doctor _____ take a month's holiday, because he needed a rest.

3   He said he would _____ his mind without consulting his wife.

4   He kindly _____ me a lift to the station, and of course I accepted.

5   Thank you for _____ the machine works. We are very grateful.

6   The detective _____ stealing the money.

7   He said there was no proof that he had been involved, and _____ anything to do with the affair.

8   It was a good thing you _____ post the pools coupon. We've won a hundred pounds!

9   I saw the children playing near the quarry and _____ do so, because they could easily fall in.

10 It was clear that we were not going to reach agreement, so Sally _____ put off a decision until the next meeting.

[24] 175

Phrasal verbs: *mixed*

■ Rewrite the sentences, substituting the verb in brackets at the end of each in the correct tense, together with the correct preposition, for the words printed in italics. The exercise includes some of the most common phrasal verbs that have not appeared in previous exercises.

1   I knew nothing about it, and John will *confirm* what I have been saying. (**bear**)

2   The days *grow shorter* in November. (**close**)

3   I was talking to a friend, but the operator *broke the connection between* us. (**cut**)

4   Unless we can prevent people from hunting these animals, they will *become extinct*. (**die**)

5   Have you *compiled* a list of points for us to discuss at the conference? (**draw**)

6   I don't think the possibility of our refusing had *formed part of* their calculations. (**enter**)

7   My mother would have come to the wedding, but she didn't *have the strength to make* the journey. (**feel**) (two prepositions)

8   *Don't let go of* your ticket! You'll need it later. (**hang**) (two prepositions)

9   The shelf fell on his head and *rendered him unconscious*. (**knock**)

10 This is the price *established* by the manufacturers. (**lay**)

11 You can rely on me. I won't *fail to fulfil my obligations to* you. (**let**)

12 It was a terrible scandal. I doubt if the family will ever *overcome the disgrace*. (**live**) (Use 'it'.)

13 Unfortunately, the play did not *fulfil our expectations*. (**live**) (two prepositions)

14 He was frequently interrupted at the beginning of his speech, but once the police arrived, the meeting *proceeded to its conclusion* without further incident. (**pass**)

15 We have spent a lot of money on the hotel so we hope it will *prove a successful investment*. (**pay**)

16 The train *increased* speed as we left the station. (**pick**)

17 He agreed to lecture here next year, but I couldn't *make* him *commit himself* to a firm date. (**pin**)

18 There is a rumour that a number of ministers are going to be replaced, but the official spokesman is *minimising its importance*. (**play**) (Use 'it'.)

19 The thieves have *successfully carried out* one of the most daring robberies of the century. (**pull**)

20 His lecture was mainly about 'Hamlet', but he also *mentioned* 'Macbeth' *briefly*. (**touch**)

[24] 176

Rephrasing

■ For each of the sentences, write a new sentence as similar as possible in meaning to the original sentence, but using the word given. This word must *not* be altered in any way.

1   What I like most about Constable's work is its
    straightforwardness. (**appeals**)
2   He did not feel a need to add anything to what
    he had said before. (**necessary**)
3   He assumes that we will all support him
    (**granted**)
4   Does he know about the change in the
    situation? (**aware**)
5   I agree with you to a certain extent. (**point**)
6   They haven't got much money at the
    moment. (**short**)
7   His style of painting is old-fashioned. (**date**)
8   I'm afraid we have no copies of the book you
    are looking for in the shop. (**stock**)
9   The rebels were executed. (**death**)
10 This example completes the exercise. (**end**)
    (Not 'ends'.)

[24] 177

Sentence completion: final revision of tenses

■   Complete the sentences below with a suitable word
    or phrase.

1   I _____ so hard all morning that I feel
    worn out.
2   You needn't worry about the operation.
    You'll be asleep while the doctors
    _____.
3   If we hadn't taken our umbrellas, we
    _____.
4   I can't drive a car yet, but I _____ when
    I have passed the test.
5   Should anyone _____ a better offer,
    we'd be grateful if you'd let us know.
6   I wish you _____ while I'm working.
    It's very irritating.
7   I _____ her when she rang me instead.
8   Of course he needn't have told you about it.
    He _____ silent.
9   It's a pity you weren't there. You _____
    what he said when I told him the news.
10 I'm sorry, but I don't know _____
    about. Are you sure you dialled the right
    number?

Section 5: Selective cloze

Introduction

The first question in the Use of English paper consists of a passage, with 20 spaces left blank. You have to fill in the blanks, using one word for each space, and no more.

When you do such tests, you must remember two things, above all. First, read the whole passage carefully before you attempt to answer any of the questions. The correct word for the blank space may depend on the context of the whole sentence or paragraph. Secondly, make up your mind what sort of word is needed. In this connection, it is worth bearing in mind that most of the words missing are structural words and prepositions. Nouns are rare and adjectives almost never appear, because in such cases too many possibilities are available. The test is not a test of vocabulary, but of your ability to recognise the way sentences are formed in English.

[1] 178

■ Study this paragraph from an essay on the novel *Heart of Darkness* and decide what sort of word is needed to complete the gaps in each case. Then compare your ideas with the notes below before choosing the correct words to complete the paragraph.

Joseph Conrad, _____(1) author of *Heart of Darkness*, used _____(2) own experience as the captain of a steamer _____(3) the river Congo in _____(4) the book. From the beginning of the story, the narrator, Marlow, _____(5) stands for Conrad himself, _____(6) us see that the Romans looked at the Britons in the same way _____(7) modern Europeans regard the natives in Africa. _____(8) is not so _____(9) difference between civilisation and savagery _____(10) people imagine.

Notes: 1) definite article 2) possessive adjective 3) preposition 4) gerund, following a preposition 5) relative pronoun 6) verb – which tense? Note the infinitive form, **see**, which depends on it and has no **to** before it 7) a structural word, depending on **the same** 8) the beginning of a sentence – is it **It**, an impersonal

subject, or **There**, indicating the existence, or in negative form, lack of existence of something? 9) not an adjective like **great** (not such a **great** difference), but a form relating to number 10) making a comparison.

[1] 179

In this paragraph, all the missing words are either prepositions or relative pronouns (**that**, **which**, etc.) or adverbs (**where**, etc.).

■ Read the paragraph carefully before deciding on the correct word to fill each space.

It is curious that Joseph Conrad, _____(1) novels are now regarded as _____(2) the greatest ever written _____(3) English, was _____(4) fact born _____(5)Poland, and English was his fourth language. Conrad, _____(6) real name was Konrad Korzeniowski, grew up _____(7) a time when Poland was divided _____(8) Russia, Germany and the Austro–Hungarian Empire. His father, _____(9) had been a famous Polish patriot, died as a prisoner _____(10) Russian hands, and Conrad was brought _____(11) by his uncle. As the son of a political prisoner, he was liable _____(12) 25 years' military service in Russia, and so, _____(13) the age of 17, he went to France, _____(14) he joined the French merchant navy. Later, the realisation _____(15) he could never become an officer caused him to leave France. He arrived _____(16) England _____(17) knowing much English, _____(18) nevertheless did not prevent him _____(19) rising to the rank of captain and eventually writing his great novels, many of _____(20) are about the sea.

[2] 180

The majority of the words missing in this paragraph are either words that form part of connectors, as in (1), and structural words. Where a verb is missing, as in (6), consider the verb that is *usually* found in connection with the noun, in this case **complaints**, or else, as in

(7), take into account which verbs are normally followed by a preposition (in this case, **to**), gerund or infinitive construction.

■ Read the paragraph carefully before deciding on the correct word to fill each space.

_____(1) to Thomas Carlyle, work is the main reason _____(2) our existence. On the other _____(3), many people dream _____(4) winning the pools or the lottery and retiring. But in _____(5) of the complaints that people _____(6) about their jobs, their work always _____(7) to them. When we start a conversation with strangers, we _____(8) talk about the weather or ask them _____(9) they do. _____(10) theory, they could reply: 'I eat, drink and sleep,' but in _____(11), they understand the question. If they are out of _____(12), they may answer that they are not doing _____(13) at the moment. In _____(14) words, 'doing' means the same thing _____(15) 'working' in this conversation, and work has so _____(16) importance for us that when someone says he is unemployed we do not know _____(17) to go on with the conversation. In these _____(18), it is not surprising that people would _____(19) do unpleasant jobs than do no work _____(20) all.

[3] 181

■ Read the paragraph carefully before deciding on the correct word to fill each space.

The development of country parks in England has been taking _____(1) so quietly and so _____(2) fuss has been _____(3) about it that many people are unaware of _____(4) has been achieved. If you go to a country park you _____(5) not expect to find anything _____(6) big as a national park, or, _____(7) the other hand, anything as _____(8) as the local recreation ground. Country parks come somewhere between the _____(9), with an emphasis _____(10) leisure rather _____(11) conservation. Ten years _____(12), the country park was _____(13) more than _____(14) idea proposed in a Government White Paper _____(15) *Leisure in the Countryside*. Today _____(16) are well _____(17) 100 country parks in nearly _____(18) corner of England and Wales, and more parks are _____(19) to be opened _____(20) the future.

[4] 182

■ Read the paragraph carefully before deciding on the correct word to fill each space.

_____(1) has been government policy _____(2) many years to provide disabled people _____(3) a vehicle known _____(4) a tricycle _____(5) they lack the ability to handle the controls. The increasing number of accidents caused _____(6) the bad design of this vehicle has _____(7) to various governments _____(8) denying that it was unsafe; secondly, admitting that the design _____(9) the vehicle unsafe but arguing that they were _____(10) to do anything about it because it was the _____(11) possible solution to the problem; finally, preventing disabled people _____(12) using tricycles _____(13) their own interest. The last decision is the _____(14) currently _____(15) reviewed. Of _____(16), if there are adequate funds any difficulty can be overcome, but _____(17) spending more money _____(18) is spent _____(19) present, disabled people could be provided with vehicles _____(20) safe as the four-wheeled equivalents.

[5] 183

■ Read the paragraph carefully before deciding on the correct word to fill each space.

What _____(1) of food are we _____(2) to be eating in the year 2000? Most people, when you _____(3) them a question _____(4) that, either say: '_____(5) won't be any left,' or '_____(6) it is, it won't be _____(7) eating.' There are good reasons _____(8) people are pessimistic about the world's food supplies. On the other _____(9) not all the experts share the general despondency. For _____(10) thing, although population is _____(11) fast, food production, _____(12) least in Europe, _____(13) to be rising, too. The problem is not _____(14) much that there is a world food shortage _____(15) that methods of cultivation are _____(16) old-fashioned in many parts of the world and the food is not fairly distributed to all _____(17) that need it. _____(18) from that, many governments are interested in _____(19) their farmers happy and would rather _____(20) the food be destroyed than force them to lower their prices.

[6] 184

- Read the paragraph carefully before deciding on the correct word to fill each space.

It is often said that wide reading is the best _____(1) of action _____(2) advanced students of English to follow if they want to _____(3) their English, but even _____(4) that is a sensible suggestion it is necessary to _____(5) some sort of selection. It is no _____(6) telling students to go to the library and _____(7) the first book they come _____(8). My own advice to them is: 'read _____(9) you can understand _____(10) having to look up words in a dictionary (but not what you can understand at a _____(11); read what you have time _____(12) (magazines and newspapers _____(13) than novels, _____(14) you can read a novel in a week or so; read the English written today, not 200 years _____(15); read _____(16) much as you can and try to remember _____(17) it was written, _____(18) is more important than worrying about words that you did not recognise.' Of course, _____(19) of saying 'read', I could just as _____(20) say 'listen to'.

[7] 185

- Read the paragraphs carefully before deciding on the correct word to fill each space.

Research _____(1) out at the University of Newcastle shows that most dam failures occur _____(2) within the first _____(3) years after construction or after a long uneventful period of operation. It _____(4) that many of Britain's dams are now approaching the _____(5) stage. A _____(6) of incidents have occurred which _____(7) or may not lead to collapse but which certainly call _____(8) remedial action to be _____(9) into effect. If the present trend continues, we may expect an increase _____(10) such events and, _____(11) or later, a failure.

The relatively good safety record of British dams _____(12) doubt stems from sound engineering practice but might also be partly _____(13) to luck. _____(14) now, authorities have _____(15) been prosecuted for failing to repair a dam, and _____(16) when they have, the penalties have been mild. _____(17), some dams have never been inspected, _____(18) there is an obligation to do so. The risk of _____(19) so many different local authorities responsible for dams is that it could result _____(20) standards of safety that vary widely throughout the country.

[8] 186

- Read the paragraph carefully before deciding on the correct word to fill each space.

The western suffered a serious decline _____(1) the 1970s. _____(2) westerns were made, and those few were not very good _____(3) particularly successful. The old westerns depended to a considerable extent _____(4) a mythical view of the past, _____(5) these newer films tried to undermine. _____(6) the old films, the films of the seventies _____(7) a clear alternative version of the west, _____(8) that was more realistic. _____(9) a result, the western was no _____(10) familiar and soothing, _____(11) an old slipper, and this _____(12) adjustment to it difficult, if not impossible. Once the loyal audience became _____(13) loyal, film-makers understandably _____(14) interest _____(15) the genre. What is interesting about the article _____(16) page 45 that deals _____(17) this subject, however, is the argument _____(18) forward that Americans saw _____(19) at one time as the natural successors of the people in westerns, but do not do so _____(20) more.

[9] 187

- Read the paragraph carefully before deciding on the correct word to fill each space.

Monkeys and chimpanzees, _____(1) they are weaker and _____(2) fierce than many other animals, possess brains which are as _____(3) along the evolutionary road as any creature _____(4) than man. Birds are _____(5) of extraordinary feats of technical skill, but they _____(6) think or reason. The abilities they possess are instincts derived _____(7) their genetic inheritance. Monkeys, _____(8) the other hand, can easily remember where food is to be _____(9) and what kind of food they are looking _____(10). If one _____(11) a monkey a problem, _____(12) that of reaching a banana high up in its cage, it will work out some system for _____(13) hold of it. It is _____(14) that the psychologist, Wolfgang Köhler, once provided a chimpanzee

_____(15) equipment in _____(16) to test _____(17) ability to work out a method for _____(18) a fruit. The animal used Köhler _____(19) as the quickest means of getting to the fruit. I _____(20) I had been there to see Köhler's face when this happened.

[10] 188

■ Read the paragraph carefully before deciding on the correct word to fill each space.

Like Great Britain, Japan is an island, or _____(1), a number of islands, and _____(2) a result of the rapid growth of its population and the consequent pollution, _____(3) of its problems are _____(4) to ours. _____(5) the same, it has more serious natural hazards to _____(6) with than we have. It lies on a point _____(7) two continental plates meet, _____(8) that there is a constant risk of earthquakes. Tokyo shares with San Francisco the unenviable reputation of _____(9) a city certain to suffer _____(10) the future _____(11) an earthquake like the _____(12) that killed thousands of people _____(13) 1923. To _____(14) matters worse, the land has subsided _____(15) then, and 60 sq. km. of the Tokyo city area are now _____(16) sea level, with the consequent risks of widespread flooding, _____(17) is in any _____(18) a perennial hazard in Japan. Anyone _____(19) at Japan's technological achievement in the light of these statements cannot help _____(20) of it with a mixture of admiration and sympathy.

[11] 189

■ Read the paragraph carefully before deciding on the correct word to fill each space.

Even _____(1) the World Wildlife Fund regards the Copal factory near Lake Nakuru _____(2) a serious threat to wild life, it does not believe that the factory is to _____(3) for the recent departure of the flamingoes from the lake. _____(4) to now, the copper effluent from the factory has not _____(5) had time to have a serious effect _____(6) the algae that provide the basis for the birds' food chain. In _____(7) case, Lake Nakuru is only one of several temporary homes used _____(8) the birds. Now that the flamingoes have begun to return to the lake _____(9) large numbers,

however, the risk _____(10) again arises of the algae dying and the majority of the birds departing for _____(11). The destruction of the lake could be justified if the commercial exploitation of its resources _____(12) of great importance to Kenya. But the company's operations _____(13) little sense. If most of its output is intended for export, what is the _____(14) of building the factory _____(15) far from the coast, _____(16) means that both raw materials and finished products have to make expensive journeys? The advantages of the Copal operation are _____(17) to prove, and cannot be compared to the damage that will be _____(18) to the lake. _____(19) is still time to prevent the damage _____(20) becoming irreparable, but it is fast running out.

[12] 190

■ Read the paragraph carefully before deciding on the correct word to fill each space.

The Swiss mountain farmers are a special breed of men. They work for at _____(1) twelve hours _____(2) day in conditions that _____(3) it very difficult to cultivate anything and that _____(4) animals can _____(5) up to. Many of the farmers work at some other _____(6), too, leaving their wives and children to _____(7) most of the farm work. In _____(8) of all the difficulties inherent in working in the Swiss mountains, why should anyone object to the economy _____(9) strengthened by tourism? The reason is that people are _____(10) of the farms disappearing _____(11) a result. Switzerland needs its mountain farmers because they contribute _____(12) the food supply in a country that is only _____(13) of producing 45 per cent of its requirements; the neat Swiss landscape, _____(14) attracts the tourists, could be not maintained _____(15) them; _____(16) to them, the fields are fertilised and the woods are _____(17) for. If the landscape and the mountains are to be preserved all _____(18) of agricultural enterprise _____(19) be encouraged, and the farmers form a necessary _____(20) of this enterprise.

[13] 191

■ Read the paragraph carefully before deciding on the correct word to fill each space.

King Edward VII _____(1) up to be a popular, successful king, _____(2) is remarkable when _____(3) considers his appalling childhood. He was educated in isolation and not _____(4) the companionship of other boys and girls. Nevertheless, he _____(5) to serve a long apprenticeship before _____(6) king; he was Prince of Wales _____(7) forty years _____(8) his mother, Queen Victoria, reigned, always in mourning for her husband, the Prince Consort. The Queen was _____(9) of her son, _____(10) real name was Albert, _____(11) his father's, but blamed his behaviour _____(12) her husband's early death. When she died at _____(13) in 1901, the new king was nearly 60, but he enjoyed the job so _____(14) that he did not seem _____(15) as old. He was quite successful in foreign policy; he _____(16) peace with Russia and discouraged his nephew, the German Emperor, _____(17) starting a war. _____(18) made him popular at home was that he seemed good-humoured; the people did not _____(19) him having a succession of mistresses, and his horses nearly always won, so ordinary people made quite a lot of money betting _____(20) them.

[14] 192

■ Read the paragraph carefully before deciding on the correct word to fill each space.

The success rate of up to 90% claimed for lie detectors is attractive _____(1) misleading. Before we accept the proposal that they _____(2) be introduced into British companies _____(3) widely as in the United States, _____(4) us imagine a company with 500 employees, twenty of _____(5) are thieves. In _____(6) a situation, the machine could catch 18 of them but _____(7) doing so would place _____(8) more under suspicion, because in one case in _____(9) ten it would _____(10) a mistake. The problem for the management would therefore become _____(11) of deciding how _____(12) industrial unrest it was prepared to cause in _____(13) to eliminate theft. It seems surprising that a simpler method of using lie detectors has not yet _____(14) into fashion.

_____(15) of asking suspected persons to answer questions, this method requires that they _____(16) read aloud statements about the crime _____(17) question. Clearly, anyone who knew _____(18) about the crime would not _____(19) any distinction between saying: 'The thief was wearing a sports jacket', and 'The thief was _____(20) in a blue suit.' The guilty might escape, but the innocent would not be wrongly arrested.

[15] 193

■ Read the paragraph carefully before deciding on the correct word to fill each space.

The author of the article _____(1) *Liberty v. Equality* on page 50 argues that segregation according _____(2) ability did almost _____(3) much to promote class division in Britain as the traditional division _____(4) state and private schools, based _____(5) money and social class. In his attempt to reconcile justice and freedom, he uses _____(6) an example the schools of the Scottish borders, where _____(7) child received the same education, _____(8) was of high quality. He is concerned that local authorities nowadays, interested _____(9) all in equality, prevent parents _____(10) exercising any choice at all, and suggests that parents should be _____(11) a choice, provided this did not have a bad effect _____(12) the system. He paints an idealistic picture of a community in _____(13) one school has a reputation for athletics, _____(14) for a permissive style of education, and a third for _____(15) music. The trouble _____(16) this is that in real life parents, if they were given this opportunity, _____(17) be more _____(18) to base their choice on the fact that one school had a much _____(19) academic record than the others, or that another school was built in the nineteenth century and was on the _____(20) of falling down!

[16] 194

■ Read the paragraph carefully before deciding on the correct word to fill each space.

Officially, _____(1) should be no such county _____(2) Middlesex, because it was decided _____(3) 1963, when the Greater London Council was set _____(4), that in future it _____(5) be administered from London. The inhabitants were not in _____(6) of the change at the time, presumably because they realised that a larger local authority would _____(7) less attention to _____(8) particular needs. Now, for reasons that have very _____(9) to do _____(10) Middlesex, the Government has proposed that there should no _____(11) be a Greater London Council. If this proposal _____(12) law, the question _____(13) of what will happen to Middlesex. No _____(14) civil servants will argue that it is not just a simple matter of restoring boundaries and responsibilities _____(15) the original county administration, which is no longer _____(16) existence. But it is pleasant to think that Middlesex, _____(17) been buried by bureaucracy twenty years _____(18), should now _____(19) again from the ashes and once more be considered fit to run its _____(20) affairs!

[17] 195

■ Read the paragraph carefully before deciding on the correct word to fill each space.

Is _____(1) any truth in astrology? Interest _____(2) it has certainly increased in Britain in recent years, _____(3) more than half of the population admit to _____(4) at the daily forecasts for their sign of the zodiac in the _____(5). In the _____(6) way, books _____(7) the subject to the general public in simple terms have sold over a million _____(8). To be fair, it is _____(9) pointing out that a professional astrologer would laugh _____(10) the idea of there _____(11) any connection _____(12) popular newspaper forecasts and individual natal charts, which _____(13) to interpret personality, temperament and abilities according _____(14) the positions of the planets _____(15) the exact moment of a person's _____(16). It is hardly likely, to take a simple example, that one person in _____(17) twelve will inherit money _____(18) the same day. Most people, of course, believe the _____(19) if it _____(20) them what they want to hear, and ignore it if it doesn't.

[18] 196

■ Read the paragraph carefully before deciding on the correct word to fill each space.

From the beginning of history, people _____(1) considered gold to be the _____(2) precious of metals, but it was not _____(3) the nineteenth century that gold rushes in _____(4) of it spread all over the globe. Those who took _____(5) in the first of these, to California in 1848, had to _____(6) the dangerous journey across the Rocky Mountains or go _____(7) sea round Cape Horn. The _____(8) conditions of all, however, were _____(9) that prospectors encountered in Alaska and the Klondike _____(10) the end of the century. It has been calculated that over 100,000 people _____(11) out for Alaska, of _____(12) only 40,000 arrived and perhaps 4,000 found gold. _____(13) then, there were very _____(14) among this small minority who made a fortune. Nowadays the principal source of gold is South Africa, _____(15) it was first found about 100 years ago, but there are _____(16) thousands of mining claims _____(17) worked in the Klondike. Surprising _____(18) this may seem, it is understandable when we learn that if all the gold that has _____(19) been found were melted together, it would only form a cube six metres long _____(20) each side.

[19] 197

■ Read the paragraph carefully before deciding on the correct word to fill each space.

Social psychologists have started to analyse walking _____(1) a skilled performance. The main problem is _____(2) of navigation; how are we _____(3) to avoid collisions? As we see other people coming _____(4) us, we must first decide who is walking together and who is on his _____(5). Convention dictates that the solitary _____(6) must recognise the unity of an approaching group and walk round it; to do _____(7) is considered rude. If the group is _____(8) big to allow this, it usually _____(9) up into smaller units to _____(10) the lone walker pass. People walking together show that they are _____(11) so in a number of ways. They may be _____(12) hands or talking to _____(13) other, but the _____(14) reliable sign of togetherness is that they stay close to one another. This is obvious when they _____(15) a corner; by slowing down or waiting _____(16) another person, pedestrians _____(17) it clear that they are walking _____(18), and not merely _____(19) the same pavement _____(20) the same speed.

[20] 198

■ Read the paragraph carefully before deciding on the correct word to fill each space.

_____(1) do you react to a flag-seller in the street? Do you hurry past _____(2) the other side? _____(3) are you one of the people who buy flags willingly? _____(4) category you fall into, there is _____(5) doubt that attitudes towards flag days have changed over the years. Flag days had _____(6) beginnings in Britain in 1912 and grew rapidly during the First World War, _____(7) a great deal of money was raised by this method. Today, perhaps as a _____(8) of adverse criticism by people _____(9) approached by too _____(10) charities, flag days are limited in London _____(11) four _____(12) year. Local authorities are given six weeks in _____(13) one year for work of this _____(14). Most of them still give preference to local causes, suggesting that charity begins _____(15) home. _____(16) is probably for this reason that alternative means of fund raising are becoming popular. Oxfam _____(17) the lead in selling direct to the public from shops. Ironically, a few charity emblems were recently _____(18) to Oxfam, and items that originally _____(19) only a few pence were put on _____(20) to collectors at a much higher price.

[21] 199

■ Read the paragraph carefully before deciding on the correct word to fill each space.

Anyone who glances at the financial pages of British newspapers is bound to _____(1) across the term 'take-over-bid'. He may also _____(2) about 'mergers', _____(3) in practice _____(4) to very much the same sort of thing. The only difference is _____(5) of emphasis. A merger suggests two companies joining forces for their mutual benefit, while a take-over implies one company _____(6) control of the other _____(7) the other likes it or not. At one time, the Government _____(8) to favour take-overs on the _____(9) that the _____(10) a company is, the more competitive it will be abroad. This analysis overlooks some disadvantages, _____(11) all because _____(12) one has worked _____(13) systematically why the majority of mergers take _____(14). A company taking over another may really want to

_____(15) up a strong combination _____(16) of resisting foreign competition but it is just _____(17) likely to be interested _____(18) eliminating a smaller, _____(19) efficient rival, _____(20) presence in the home market is embarrassing.

[22] 200

■ Read the paragraph carefully before deciding on the correct word to fill each space.

An elderly woman died last week after _____(1) knocked down by a motorist who had _____(2) no attempt to brake. A police sergeant asked the driver, a man _____(3) 69, to read the number-plate of a car parked not _____(4) away. The man said this was unfair, because it was foggy, although in fact the sun was _____(5). After several attempts, even from a distance of two metres, the man _____(6) failed to read a number-plate correctly. He said he had never _____(7) glasses, though he had been _____(8) in a similar accident a _____(9) days earlier. The question of fitness to _____(10) comes up every time some medical condition _____(11) to an accident like this. A month or so ago verdicts of accidental death were returned on two motorists, both of _____(12) died _____(13) a result of _____(14) consciousness at the wheel. The first, a man _____(15) car hit a tree, had _____(16) from blackouts for years. The _____(17) died when his sports car crashed _____(18) high speed. He had a brain disease that affected _____(19) eyesight when he had a headache. With _____(20) cases in mind, it is not surprising that stricter controls for drivers are being demanded.

[23] 201

■ Read the paragraph carefully before deciding on the correct word to fill each space.

For at _____(1) 15 years people have been saying that Greenwich was _____(2) to 'come up', that its air of decay would give _____(3) to a new era of residential popularity and commercial prosperity. One project which, with _____(4), will be complete for the next tourist season and for _____(5) everyone will be _____(6) to the Greater London Council, is the modernisation of the Pier. The Council _____(7) that it has spent £93,000 _____(8) it. _____(9) a result, visitors

will no _____(10) have to wait in the rain for
river boats back to London. They will now be
_____(11) to wait under cover, and
_____(12) is more, not _____(13) the
risk of getting lost while looking for the right boat,
_____(14) to a new destination board near the
pier entrance. This pleases Mr Herbert Snowball,
who has struggled for _____(15) five years to
obtain permission to import hydrofoils
_____(16) Russia. The hydrofoils will provide
travellers _____(17) a 10-minute journey to
London _____(18) 10-minute intervals, which
is a _____(19) service than the railway has
_____(20) given in 140 years of operation.

[24] 202

■ Read the paragraph carefully before deciding on
the correct word to fill each space.

_____(1) the majority of artists of his time,
Constable had _____(2) faith in 'inspiration'.
_____(3) the contrary, he simply painted
what he saw. In _____(4) of his
straightforward response to nature, however, he
was guilty of _____(5) public taste to
_____(6) an influence on him, _____(7)
that his private work is not only different
_____(8) what he exhibited, but considerably
better. He seems to _____(9) regarded art
_____(10) a profession that would
_____(11) him respectability and
_____(12) money to look _____(13) his
family, and _____(14) more. He even judged
his success in _____(15) of money, not fame.
We are still _____(16) deeply influenced by
the romantic idea of the artist that we may
_____(17) this strange. To some
_____(18), we accept the romantic artist's
conviction that the world _____(19) him a
living. Until the beginning of the nineteenth
century, most artists thought they had to
_____(20) a living for themselves.

Test Papers

Test 1 (Two hours)

Section A

1   *Fill each of the numbered blanks in the following passage with **one** suitable word.*

The cuckoo is _____ (1) is called a brood parasite. _____ (2) is to say, it _____ (3) its eggs in the nests of other birds, which _____ (4) as foster parents to the young cuckoos. Although the eggs of the host species are often _____ (5) different colours, there is always a similarity in appearance between the cuckoo's eggs and _____ (6) of the host. A female cuckoo normally leaves only one of its eggs in each host nest and takes away _____ (7) of the host's, _____ (8) sure that the same number will remain _____ (9) there were in the first _____ (10). If birds notice a strange egg in the nest, they _____ (11) build another nest on _____ (12) of the first, or else _____ (13) with the problem by getting _____ (14) of the strange egg. But cuckoos rarely make the _____ (15) of leaving their eggs in a nest that _____ (16) to the wrong host. We do not know _____ (17) the cuckoo learns to distinguish suitable nests _____ (18) it somehow results from the female cuckoo being _____ (19) up by foster parents of a similar species. The most remarkable feature of the process is that so _____ (20) cuckoo eggs are lost, only 8% of the total.

2   *Finish each of the following sentences in such a way that it means exactly the same as the sentence printed before it.*

EXAMPLE   I expect that he will get there by lunch-time.

ANSWER   I expect him *to get there by lunch-time.*

a)   It's a pity I didn't write down her address.
   I wish _____

b)   She dropped the milk jug and, as she did so, spilt the milk on the carpet.
   She dropped the milk jug and, in _____

c)   I will not sign a binding contract under any circumstances.
   Under no circumstances _____

d)   Don't tell him about it, whatever happens.
   He _____

e)   There's no reason why they should object, as far as I can see.
   There's no reason for _____

f)   It would be a shame to leave them behind.
   Let's _____

g)   I'm not bothered about it. It's Harold that's getting upset.
   I'm not bothered about it. Harold _____

h)   Whenever he went back to Farley, he was reminded of his happy childhood there.
   He never _____

i)   He said it was my fault, which was unkind.
   It was _____

j)   Perhaps he didn't see the note you left on the table.
   He may _____

3   *Fill each of the blanks with a suitable word or phrase.*

EXAMPLE   Even if I had stood on a chair, *I wouldn't have been able to* reach the light bulb.

a)   Where have you been? I _____ you everywhere.

b)   When you _____ as many examinations as I have, you won't feel nervous.

c)   If you _____ to her so rudely, she wouldn't have got upset.

d)   'He may have put them back while you weren't looking.' 'He _____. They'd be there now.'

e)   I'm sorry to _____ waiting such a long time. I was held up by the traffic.

f)   Only when I had read the message a second time _____ what it meant.

g)   _____ truth, I don't think you know what you're talking about.

h)   They've given him the job but I doubt if he _____ doing it well.

i)   It's been a lovely evening, but now it's time _____ home.

j)   I'm going to tell him what I think of him, whether he _____.

4   *For each of the sentences, write a new sentence **as similar as possible in meaning to the original sentence**, but using the word given. This word must not be altered in any way.*

EXAMPLE John inflated the tyres of his bicycle.
blew

ANSWER *John blew up the tyres of his bicycle.*

a) He's lived here since the day he was born.
life

_____

b) Did you manage to finish the job?
succeed

_____

c) I assume you will be at the meeting tonight.
granted

_____

d) The new plan cannot be implemented immediately.
effect

_____

e) Did he explain why he behaved like that?
reason

_____

f) His father thought what he had done was wrong.
approve

_____

g) It's no use losing your temper.
point

_____

h) You shouldn't take any notice of what she says.
attention

_____

i) I don't think there will be enough food for everyone.
go round

_____

j) These problems must also be considered.
taken

_____

Section B

5 Read the following passage, then answer the questions that follow it.

One result of government rethinking on transport spending, combined with hard pruning of capital spending in the public sector, is clearly going to be that local councils, like central government, will build fewer new roads. One by-product of this situation may prove positive; it may stimulate fresh action and free the relatively small sums of money needed to improve the lot of the pedestrian.

Until the late 1960s efforts to take the traffic out of places where people shopped or strolled or wished to linger for pleasure seemed dogged by delay and obstruction. A few shopping precincts had been created in the centres of new towns or blitzed cities – Coventry was a pioneer – but other cities, like Bristol, were prevented from doing so by the threat of boycott by developers and traders. The high street had traditionally been both market-place and thoroughfare. Shopkeepers clung to the belief that profits were made from passing trade. The fact that, in a high street congested by ever-increasing numbers of motor vehicles, car-driving shoppers were unlikely to be able to stop, was only belatedly appreciated.

But there was also a planners' mythology growing up round 'pedestrianization'. One tenet of it said that traffic-free streets must be totally free at all times of all traffic – except perhaps for fire engines, ambulances and invalid carriages. That view of footstreets is the reason why the little cathedral city of Chichester, which had its proposals for taking traffic out of the four streets that meet at the cross endorsed in the mid 60s, has still not achieved a single yard of it. Implementation waits on 99 per cent rear servicing, which involves carving lorry access routes through the historic quadrants behind the four main streets – a slow, costly and controversial process. The pioneer British scheme, at London Street in Norwich, did not wait on such perfectionist provision. Deliveries there come mainly from unloading bays at the two ends of the narrow service road that wriggles across it halfway along. The then city planning officer of Norwich, Alfred Wood, took parties of traders to the Continent to see how the Germans and the Scandinavians throve on footstreets. They enjoyed themselves, were impressed, but remained curiously sceptical of whether it would work in Britain. Then sewer works closed London Street. Some say Mr Wood arranged for them to be somewhat protracted. The months when the street was closed to traffic sufficed to convince the traders – mostly in specialist and luxury goods rather than convenience shopping – that the attractions to customers of being able to linger and look without harassment from traffic outweighed the loss of the 'carriage trade'. The traders supported an official experimental closure; turnover rose and eventually the street was paved over and landscaped, with seats, trees, and a 'sleeping policeman', a concrete ramp to slow delivery vans on the transverse service road. Norwich was praised, quoted and photographed, but for several years no one else seemed to be following its example. Then, suddenly, at the beginning of the 1970s, footstreets began to blossom in towns, large and small, all over the country. Some have managed complete rear servicing without excessive cost or damage or delay – King's Lynn with its 900 yards of traffic-free shopping streets, old and new, is a good example. Others have judged that provision of rear access to all premises would be, in terms of cost, delay

75 and difficulty, frankly not worth the candle.

Of these, certainly the most impressive is the Leeds paved zone – ¾ mile of existing shopping streets, originally much congested by through and stopping traffic, now transformed into a

80 civilized and attractive environment for the shopper. London Street, Norwich, did not provide rear servicing to all premises; goods were carried or trolleyed to shops. Leeds went one stage further. The streets were paved over from wall to

85 wall and private cars excluded under powers obtained in the 1966 Leeds Corporation Act. But lorries and other delivery vehicles were allowed in, initially at all times. The effect of the paving and accompanying landscaping and street furni-

90 ture, however, was to give people on foot confidence to stroll and wander over the whole of the street. Pedestrian primacy had been established; lorries and vans were there on sufferance. Their drivers instinctively inched forward at walking

95 pace, and stopped if their paths were blocked by people on foot.

a) What is meant by a 'by-product' (line 6)?

b) Why is it likely that sums of money will soon become available for schemes helping pedestrians?

c) What does 'so' refer to in line 17?

d) What is meant by 'passing trade' in line 21?

e) Why were many people opposed to shopping streets where traffic was not allowed?

f) What has prevented the Council in Chichester from introducing traffic-free streets in the city?

g) What does 'it' refer to in line 34?

h) And what does 'it' refer to in line 43?

i) How were traders in Norwich convinced that traffic-free streets were an advantage?

j) Why do you think the ramp is called a 'sleeping policeman' in line 62?

k) King's Lynn is referred to as 'a good example' (line 72). A good example of what?

l) What is meant by 'not worth the candle' (line 75)?

m) In what sense is it true that Leeds 'went one stage further' (lines 83–4)?

n) How were pedestrians in the Leeds paved zone given confidence to walk in the streets?

o) What does 'on sufferance' mean in line 93?

p) In a paragraph of not more than 100 words, explain how pedestrian shopping streets have become more common in English towns and cities.

Test 2 (Two hours)

Section A

1 *Fill each of the numbered blanks in the following passage with* **one** *suitable word.*

Utilitarianism is a tradition deriving from philosophers _____(1) as Bentham and Mill. Its basic principle is that _____(2) action is right if it tends to promote happiness and wrong if it has the _____(3) effect. Happiness refers here _____(4) the happiness of everyone affected by the action, not just _____(5) of the person performing it. Strictly _____(6), therefore, this is not the same _____(7) saying that a man should always _____(8) after his own interests, _____(9) some people have suggested. But it is not comparable with the majority of ethical theories, _____(10) judge acts as right and wrong automatically, without _____(11) the consequences into account. Under the heading of consequences, Utilitarians include _____(12) the good and the bad results of an action, _____(13) they arise while the action is taking _____(14) or afterwards. _____(15) to Mill, acts should be classified _____(16) morally right or wrong only if the consequences are _____(17) important that we would like to be _____(18) to force a person to act

112

in a different way and not just feel
_____(19) persuading him to
_____(20) so.

2 *Finish each of the following sentences in such a way that it means exactly the same as the sentence printed before it.*

EXAMPLE   I expect that he will get there by lunch-time.
ANSWER   I expect him *to get there by lunch-time.*

a) He asked the electors to judge him on his previous record, lest any of them should be prejudiced against him.
He asked the electors to judge him on his previous record, in case _____

b) He wasn't able to take part because he was ill.
Because of _____

c) She was wearing a new coat.
She had _____

d) Our success was due to her hard work.
It was thanks to her _____

e) They had no news of his whereabouts until last Wednesday.
It was not _____

f) 'Why didn't you look where you were going?' he said angrily.
He said: 'You should _____

g) It would be wise if you left now, before the rain starts.
You had _____

h) What I admire most about him is his honesty.
His honesty, more _____

i) We haven't heard from Susan recently.
Susan _____

j) They surrendered only when there was no hope of victory.
Only when _____

3 *Fill each of the blanks with a suitable word or phrase.*

EXAMPLE   Even if I had stood on a chair, I *wouldn't have been able to* reach the light bulb.

a) I don't know how she _____ her work done. She spends all morning gossiping.
b) I wish I _____ your advice. You were right, and I was wrong.
c) You _____ all the washing-up by yourself. I'd have helped you.
d) I didn't really want to go out with him. I'd rather _____ at home.
e) The town still looked the same to him, in spite of the changes that _____ since his childhood.
f) How extraordinary! I _____ anything like that before.

g) Had I _____ in such terrible conditions, I'd be a juvenile delinquent, too, by now.
h) It's your own fault if you didn't understand. You _____ attention to what I was saying.
i) No sooner _____ they all rushed out of class.
j) He's not _____ working at night. He's always had a daytime job before this.

4 *For each of the sentences below, write a new sentence* **as similar as possible in meaning to the original sentence***, but using the word given. This word must not be altered in any way.*

EXAMPLE   John inflated the tyres of his bicycle.
blew
ANSWER   *John blew up the tyres of his bicycle.*

a) It's difficult for me to understand it.
hardly
_____

b) Nothing frightens me.
afraid
_____

c) The court acquitted him on all counts.
guilty
_____

d) They said it was the best performance they had ever seen.
described
_____

e) I hope you don't mind me talking to you like this.
object
_____

f) I'm going to make you responsible for this department.
charge
_____

g) You've worked very well, so I'm going to raise your salary.
rise
_____

h) Why were you offended by what he said?
offence
_____

i) It will be a pleasure for us to see you next Monday.
look forward
_____

j) They have substituted plastic bottles for the old glass ones.
replaced
_____

Section B

5   Read the following passage, then answer the
    questions that follow it.

What does bird song mean? Although poets
through the ages have extolled the beauty of the
nightingale or blackbird in full voice, birds sing
not for aesthetic reasons, but because song aids
5   the individual in the cut and thrust struggle for
survival and reproduction. Birds produce a great
variety of sounds, ranging from simple croaks
and squeaks to the more complicated melodies
which are referred to as song. True song is
10 restricted to the song birds (oscines) and in
contrast to most simple call notes, such as those
given at the approach of a predator, it is largely
produced by males.

In most song birds there is rough seasonal
15 correlation between the time they begin singing
and their reproductive activities such as territory
establishment and pairing. This correlation has
led most people to assume that song is concerned
either with proclaiming territorial ownership or
20 with attracting a mate, or both, the relative
importance of the two varying from species to
species. Although these ideas seem reasonable,
there is remarkably little direct evidence for
either of the supposed functions of song. It is
25 well known for many species that a territorial
male will respond vigorously by attacking a
loudspeaker broadcasting his own species song
within his territory. This shows that a territory
owner can recognise the song of his own species
30 and identify it with a potential rival, but it does
not tell us whether song acts, as everyone has
assumed, as a deterrent to prevent intruders from
trespassing into a territory.

If song carries the simple message 'keep out',
35 why is it so complex? In most species of song
bird, each male has a repertoire of different
versions of his territorial song. Most often, the
different song types are used in the same context
and a singing male may work through his reper-
40 toire in a few hours or even minutes, so it is hard
to imagine that the different songs contain different messages. Even a small song repertoire
seems to be redundant.

Many people have speculated on the problem
45 of the significance of song repertoire. One suggestion is that varied repertoires might act as an
anti-habituation device. If a male broadcasts his
'keep-out' message again and again in the same
way, perhaps the listening intruders will even-
50 tually come to ignore it in the way that all animals
tend to wane in their response to a repetitive
stimulus, through the process of habituation. I
have found that territorial male great tits do
indeed habituate more rapidly to repetitive play-

55 back of a single song than to playback of a
repertoire. The difficulty with the habituation
argument is the assumption that habituation to
songs is an inevitable constraint on the auditory
system.
60 It is much more likely that habituation is an
adaptive phenomenon moulded by natural selection, and we know from work on many animals
that habituation to biologically important stimuli
is very slow, so why should intruders habituate to
65 the songs of territorial residents? One suggestion
is that habituation is part of the mechanism by
which intruders assess the density of birds in an
area. When a bird is trying to set up a territory in
early spring, it presumably 'shops around' look-
70 ing for a good breeding habitat where the density
of birds that have already settled is not too high.

Loudspeaker experiments show that the intruders use song as a cue for assessing density, and
habituation may be a mechanism by which an
75 intruder chooses to settle in a low density area;
the fewer song types it hears, the fewer birds are
likely to be present, and the more likely it is that
the new bird will be able to establish a territory.
So by habituating more rapidly to a smaller
80 number of song types the new settler is able to
choose a good place to settle. The advantage to
the territory holder of singing a repertoire of
songs is that he, in effect, causes the potential
new arrivals to over-estimate the density of sing-
85 ing birds and so try to settle elsewhere. This is of
course only speculation, but it should be possible
to test the idea experimentally by comparing the
response of new settlers to territories occupied
with loudspeakers playing repertoires of song
90 types and territories with single song types.

a) What does 'in full voice' mean in line 3?

_____

b) What is meant by 'the cut and thrust struggle'
    (line 5)?

_____

c) What differences are there between the sounds
    made by the oscines and other species of birds?

_____
_____

d) Why have some people assumed that song has to
    do with proclaiming territorial ownership or
    attracting a mate?

_____
_____

e) What does 'both' refer to in line 20?

_____

f) What does 'identify it with a potential rival'
    mean in line 30, and what does 'it' refer to?

_____
_____

g) What is the problem connected with the idea of a bird using song to say 'keep out' and the kind of song it sings?

_____
_____

h) What does 'habituation' mean in line 52?

_____

i) How does the writer's research seem to confirm the idea that varied repertoires act as an anti-habituation device?

_____
_____

j) What does 'shops around' mean in line 69?

_____

k) How is a repeated song likely to help a bird that wants to settle in an area?

_____
_____

l) In this context, what is meant by 'low density area' (line 75)?

_____

m) What is meant by 'territory holder' (line 82)?

_____

n) What possible solution does the writer offer for birds having a repertoire of songs?

_____
_____

o) What would prove his idea to be correct?

_____
_____

p) In a paragraph of not more than 100 words, explain why song-birds sing and why, in the writer's opinion, they use a variety of songs.

_____
_____
_____
_____
_____
_____
_____
_____

Test 3 (Two hours)

Section A

1 *Fill each of the numbered blanks in the following passage with* **one** *suitable word.*

It is fashionable among current affairs producers on radio and television to invite members of the public to the studio to express _____ (1) views. All this is _____ (2) doubt well-intentioned. The public ought to _____ (3) its views heard. But the sad

fact is that most of them are not worth _____ (4) to. Broadcasting demands considerable skill, _____ (5) is not easily learnt, so putting a lot of people _____ (6) the air who have never broadcast before usually results _____ (7) confusion. Asked for their opinions in _____ (8) of an _____ (9) of millions, people either say nothing _____ (10) pour out everyday opinions, trying hard to _____ (11) they are saying seem clever. Trying to _____ (12) this from getting out of hand, the interviewer goes from one to _____ (13). Normally he only succeeds _____ (14) cutting short the _____ (15) interesting speaker just as he or she has got going. It looks as _____ (16) the attempt to persuade the silent majority to speak only explains _____ (17) they have been silent for _____ (18) a long time. Most of them haven't _____ (19) original to _____ (20).

2 *Finish each of the following sentences in such a way that it means exactly the same as the sentence printed before it.*

EXAMPLE I expect that he will get there by lunch-time.

ANSWER I expect him *to get there by lunch-time.*

a) If he doesn't pay the rent by Saturday, I'll throw him out.
Unless _____

b) Although he hasn't been working here long, he's already impressed the manager.
He may not _____

c) It is thought that the thieves hid the money near here.
The thieves are thought _____.

d) He will not be satisfied with anything less than the full amount.
Nothing less _____

e) She was in such a terrible state that I'll never forget it.
I'll never forget what _____

f) He had no one to talk to.
There was _____

g) If she feels worse during the night, give her these tablets.
Should _____

h) I don't know how you got the idea that I'm rich.
I don't know what _____

i) Famous conductors, like Toscanini and von Karajan, have brought their orchestras here.
Such _____

j) All that prevented me from hitting him was my affection for you.
But for _____

3 *Fill each of the blanks with a suitable word or phrase.*

EXAMPLE Even if I had stood on a chair, I *wouldn't have been able to* reach the light bulb.

a) I'll ring you as soon as I _____ from my holiday.
b) Everything that _____ wrong did go wrong.
c) 'Can I do it tomorrow?'
'No, I'd rather you _____ now.'
d) It's the first time she _____ late.
e) By the time I take the examination, I _____ hundreds of examples like this.
f) Put your overcoat on in case _____ colder later on.
g) 'She last wrote to me in July.'
'Oh, so you _____ from her since then.'
h) If only I _____ coming! I'd have made a cake.
i) It was such a funny story that we couldn't stop _____.
j) The doctor suggested _____ smoking, because it was endangering his health.

4 *For each of the sentences below, write a new sentence **as similar as possible in meaning to the original sentence**, but using the word given. This word must not be altered in any way.*

EXAMPLE John inflated the tyres of his bicycle.
blew
ANSWER *John blew up the tyres of his bicycle.*

a) I demand to know what happened.
insist
b) You shouldn't let them impose on you.
advantage
c) I don't mind whether we go or not.
matter
d) I'm not to blame for it.
fault
e) He is recognized as the world's leading authority on the subject.
considered
f) Unlike you, I'm due to retire next year.
difference
g) It was reasonable to imagine I would find you here.
might
h) They share very few interests.
common

i) The play was not as good as we had expected.
live up to
j) I'm afraid that book is not available at the moment.
stock

Section B

5 Read the following passage, then answer the questions that follow it.

Two important meetings were held last summer to discuss Antarctica's resources. What is significant about these two meetings is that they involved participants from only twelve countries.

5 Why is it that, while the deep sea bed and outer space are considered the trust of the international community, the southern continent and its surrounding waters and continental shelf, over which no one has clear jurisdicition, are held to

10 be the responsibility of a privileged few?

The question is of more than academic importance. In the first place the resources at stake are significant. There are indications that Antarctica's continental shelf may contain oil and gas

15 and the waters of the Southern Ocean are rich in krill, a small crustacean, of which it is estimated that at least 50 million metric tonnes could be safely harvested annually. A number of nations are already fishing krill on an experimental basis;

20 growing population and declining supplies of food will make it increasingly difficult for others to overlook what appears to be the world's largest single source of animal protein.

Unfortunately, the environmental hazards

25 attached to the recovery of these resources may be serious. Exploitation of oil and gas would involve a number of specific dangers. A series of physical obstacles, for example, increase the likelihood of spills occurring. Large icebergs

30 which project 250 metres below the surface may damage submarine well heads, while navigational hazards increase the probability of oil spills from tankers.

Once a spill had occurred the ice would pre-

35 vent it from spreading and dissipating, and limit the use of conventional anti-pollution devices such as booms to contain it. Secondly, cold temperatures have a severe effect on the biological decomposition of oil; this slows markedly at

40 lower temperatures, with many components of the process stopping altogether in freezing water.

The ice masses and atmospheric currents in the antipodes play an important role in the world's weather and climate. It is postulated that

45 ice cover on the ocean reduces heat exchange between the atmosphere and the ocean. Seasonal and long-term variations in the extent of sea ice are thought to have a marked influence on atmos-

pheric circulation and a massive patch of polluted
50 ice could prove to be significant to the process.

Exploitation of krill itself is not without serious ecological implications. It has been iden-
tified as a principal link in the complex food
chain of the Antarctic waters and has been found
55 in the stomachs of as many as 31 different
Antarctic, sub-Antarctic, and even migratory,
sub-tropical fish species. Next to nothing is
known of the factors controlling its abundance. It
would be unwise to assume that the reduction in
60 the whale populations that grazed on krill has left
a gap that man can fill.

More direct and immediate yet than the danger
to the environment is the threat to scientific
research of resource exploitation – the recovery
65 of minerals in particular. Traditionally, Antarctica has been left to the scientists and there can be
no doubt that Antarctica's contribution to science has been considerable.

A large part of Antarctica's scientific value lies
70 in its presently undisturbed state. It provides a
unique scientific laboratory. It is clear, too, that
the restrictions on physical access which accompany exploitation will reduce the current freedom enjoyed by scientists. Companies granted
75 licences to explore given areas for a certain length
of time are hardly likely to welcome scientific
research on their doorstep, particularly if con-
ducted by scientists from a rival state. One might
also expect the secrecy that is part and parcel of
80 commercial exploration to introduce serious
limitations on the hitherto free exchange of information about the continent.

a) In what way did the meetings held last summer
   suggest that Antarctica is 'a special case'?
   _____

b) Who are the 'privileged few' referred to in
   line 10, and why are they privileged?
   _____

c) What does 'more than academic importance'
   mean in lines 11–12?
   _____

d) What is meant by 'the resources at stake'
   (line 12)?
   _____

e) Why is krill important to so many countries?
   _____

f) In what ways could the attempt to obtain oil
   and gas from Antarctica create 'environmental
   hazards' (line 24)?
   _____
   _____

g) What are 'spills' (line 29) and why would they
   be particularly dangerous in the Antarctic?
   _____

h) What does 'this' refer to in line 39?

i) What is meant by 'food chain' (lines 53–4)?

j) What sort of 'gap' is referred to in line 61 and
   why is it assumed that Man can fill it?
   _____

k) What is the value of Antarctica to the scientists
   and how is it likely to be threatened?
   _____

l) What is meant by 'the restrictions on physical
   access which accompany exploitation' (lines
   72–3)?
   _____

m) What does 'on their doorstep' mean (line 77)?
   _____

n) How are companies exploring Antarctica likely
   to react to scientists?
   _____

o) What does 'part and parcel' mean in line 79?
   _____

p) In a paragraph of not more than 100 words,
   explain the risks involved to the the ecology of
   the area in exploiting the natural resources of
   Antarctica.
   _____
   _____
   _____
   _____
   _____
   _____
   _____

Appendix

Verbs taking prepositions

This list is not complete, and does not include phrasal verbs (**look after**, **get over**, etc.). It should be used for reference to check which prepositions commonly follow a number of verbs, and also combinations of verb + noun + preposition (**take an interest in**, etc.).

Examples are given wherever more than one preposition is found after a verb with different meaning; these verbs are marked (*) and examples will be found at the end of the list.

abandon to
abbreviate to
be absent from
be absorbed in
abstain from
accede to
account for; take into account
be accountable to
accuse of; make an accusation against
be accustomed to
acquit of
act on (information)
take action on
adapt to
add to
be addicted to
adhere to
adjust to; make an adjustment to
admit to (accusation); admit to (school)
advance on
be afraid of
agree about, on, over (a matter)
agree to (an action)
agree with (another person)
be in agreement with
aim at
be allergic to
allocate to
allude to; make an allusion to
alternate with
be amazed at, by
amount to
be amused at, by
be angry at (action); with (person)
be annoyed at, about (action); with (person)
be anxious about (person, action); for (news)
apologise for (person, action) to

(another person); make an apology for (person, action) to (another person)
appeal for (help), to (person)
apply to (person) for (job); make an application to (person) for (job)
be appropriate to
approve of
argue about (subject); with (person); have an argument about (subject) with (person)
arrest for; put under arrest
ascribe to
be ashamed of (past action); be ashamed to (admit it)
ask about (person, information); ask for (person, help, etc.)
assign to
assure of; give an assurance of
be astonished at, by
attach to; be attached to
attend to; pay attention to
be aware of

bargain for (= expect); with (person); make a bargain with
beg for (thing)
believe in; have a belief in
belong to
benefit from
*bet against; on
blame for; take the blame for
boast about, of; make a boast about
borrow from

be capable of
*care about; for; take care of
cater for
centre on

be certain about, of
*change into; to; make a change in
charge for
cheat out of
choose between; make a choice between
coincide with
collaborate in (action); with (person)
combine with
comment on; make a comment on
commit to
*communicate to; with
compare with; make a comparison with
compensate for
compete against, with (person); for (prize)
complain to (person) about (thing); of (person, thing); make a complaint to (person) about
*compliment on; pay a compliment to
comply with
be composed of
compromise with
concentrate on
*be concerned about; in; with
condemn for (crime); to (punishment)
confer on (matter); with (person)
confess to
confide in
be confident about, of; have confidence in
conform to
confront with
congratulate on
be conscious of
consent to; give consent to
*consist in; of

be consistent with
consult about, on
be content with
contrast with
contribute to; make a contribution
    to
be convenient for, to
*convert into; to
convince of
cooperate with
cope with
count on
credit with; give credit for
be critical of; make criticism of
be cruel to
cure of
deal in (goods); with (matter,
    person)
decide about, on; make a decision
    about, on
dedicate to
depend on
derive from
detach from
deter from
develop into
*die from; of
differ from; make a difference to
be different from
be disappointed in; be a
    disappointment to
discourage from
dismiss from
dispose of
disqualify from
be distant from
dream about, of; have a dream
    about
dress in
be dressed in
drink to

be engaged in (business); to
    (person)
be equal to
equip with
escape from
exchange for
excuse for; from; make excuse for
*experiment on; with; make an
    experiment on; with
explain to

be familiar with
be famous for
feed on

be fond of; have a fondness for
*be free from; of; with
*be friendly towards, with; make
    friends with
be frightened of
be full of
be furious about (action); with
    (person)

be generous to (person); with
    (money)
be glad of
glance at
*be good at; for
be grateful for (action); to (person)
be guilty of

be hard on
head for
hear about, of
hope for

be ideal for
be identical with
identify with
implicate in
impose on
improve on; make improvements in
be an inconvenience to/
    inconvenient to
indulge in
infect with
infer from; make an inference from
inform of
*inject into; with
inquire into; make an inquiry into
    (matter); about (person, thing)
insert in
insist on
be interested in; take an interest in
*interfere in; with
introduce to
invest in; make an investment in
be involved in
issue to (person); with (documents)

be jealous of
join to

be keen on
be kind to

laugh about (event); laugh at
    (person, joke)
lean on
*leave to; with

lend to
be liable to
*be limited in; to
listen to
long for; have a longing for
*be lucky at; in

*be mad about; on; with
marvel at
mean by
*merge into; with
*mistake for; make a mistake about

negotiate on (matter); with (person)

object to; make an objection to
*be occupied with; in
offer to; make an offer to
operate on
*opt against; for; out of

participate in
pay for
persist in
*point at; to
be polite to
prefer to; have a preference for
be prejudiced against
prepare for
present to (person); with (thing)
protect against, from
protest against
be proud of; take pride in
*provide for; with; make provision for
punish for

quarrel about, over (matter); with
    (person)

*react against; to
be ready for
reason about, on (subject); with
    (person)
release from
relegate to
be relevant to
rely on
*remind about; of
be replaced by, with
reply to
report on (event, person); to
    (employer)
rescue from
reserve for; make a reservation for
resign from
be resigned to

*be responsible for; to; have responsibility for
*result from; in
retire from
reward for (action); with (prize)
rhyme with
get rid of
rob of

be satisfied with
save from
send for
separate from
serve with
be set on
settle with
share in (project); with (person); have a share in
shoot at; take a shot at
be short of
sigh for
signal to
be similar to
smell of
smile at

be sorry about (event); for (person, action)
specialise in
spend on
spy on
stare at
steal from
be subject to
submit to
substitute for
succeed in
suffer from
be suitable for
be superior to
supply to (person); with (goods)
be sure about, of
be surprised at, by
suspect of
be suspicious of
swear about (event); at (person)
sympathise with; be in sympathy with

talk about (person, event); to (person); have a talk to

(person); give a talk on (subject)
thank for; give thanks for
threaten with; be a threat to
be tired of
trade in (goods); with (person)
transform into
translate into
treat for (illness); with (medicine)
triumph over
*trouble about; with; take trouble over; make trouble for, with
be true of

be unaware of
be used to
be useful for (purpose); to (person)

be vital to
vote for

wait for
wonder at
work on; be at work on
worry about, over

Examples

BET   I've **bet against** him/the horse. He has **bet on** the horse.

CARE   I don't **care about** her/it any more. (I'm not worried about her/it.)
I don't **care for** her/it any more. (I don't like)
I'll **take care of** her/it. (look after)

CHANGE   I'm going to **change into** something warmer. (put on)
The witch **changed** the prince **into** a frog. (transformed)
We're **changing to** summer time tonight. (making a change from . . . to)
We've had to **make a change in** the programme.

COMMUNICATE   Would you **communicate** our deepest sympathy **to** him? (let him have)
I find it difficult to **communicate with** them. (make contact with)

COMPLIMENT   He **complimented her on** her dress.
He **paid a compliment to** her, *or* He **paid her a compliment**.

BE CONCERNED   **I'm concerned** (worried) **about** the children.
Were you **concerned in** the affair? (Did you take part in it?)
I'm not concerned with that part of the business. (It's not my responsibility.)

CONSIST   The value of the experiment **consists in** its simplicity. (is, in essence)
The experiment **consists of** three stages. (is made up of, composed of)

CONVERT   It was **converted into** a cinema. (transformed)
It was **converted to** more profitable uses. (altered)
He was **converted to** Buddhism.

DIE   He **died of** pneumonia. (Pneumonia was the cause of his death.)
He **died from** a fall. (as a result of – The fall did not kill him at the time.)

EXPERIMENT   He's **experimenting on** mice/tropical diseases. (They are the subject of his experiments.)
He's **experimenting with** mice/viruses. (making use of them in his experiments, trying to find out what will happen to them)

BE FREE	At last she **was free from** pain. (without pain) The goods **are free of** tax. (not subject to) He's **free with** his money. (doesn't take care of it, isn't careful with)
BE FRIENDLY	They **were friendly towards** the newcomers. (not unfriendly or aggressive) They **were friendly with** their neighbours. (on good terms with)
BE GOOD	She's **good at** games. (plays well, etc.) That's only **good for** practice. (useful for)
INJECT	They're going to **inject** penicillin **into** the patient. They're going to **inject** the patient **with** penicillin.
INTERFERE	I've no wish to **interfere in** the matter. I've no wish to **interfere with** you/what you're doing.
LEAVE	He **left** the money/problem **to** me. (I received it.) He **left** the money/problem **with** me. (made it my responsibility)
BE LIMITED	He's **limited in** intelligence. (not very intelligent) He's **limited to** spending £10 a day. (not allowed to spend more)
BE LUCKY	He's **lucky at** cards. (lucky when playing) He's **lucky in** love. (fortunate in general terms in)
BE MAD	He's **mad about/on** country and western music. (very fond of) He's **mad with** her. (angry)
MERGE	The waters from the river **merge into** the ocean. (become part of one greater element) The waters from the Mississippi **merge with** those of the Missouri. (join)
MISTAKE	I **mistook** you for your cousin. (thought you were, mistakenly) I'd never **make a mistake about** a thing like that.
BE OCCUPIED	He's **occupied with** a customer at the moment. (busy with) He's **occupied in** trying to work out the programme for next year. (busy)
OPT	I **opted for** the higher offer. (chose) I **opted out of** the deal. (decided not to take part in)
POINT	Don't **point at** people. It's rude. He was **pointing to** the cathedral. (indicating) (Note: **at** is used with **point, throw,** etc. to indicate aggression.)
PROVIDE	You would be wise to **provide for** the future. (make preparations for) We **provided them with** food, *or* We **provided food for** them. (supplied)
REACT	Naturally, we **reacted against** such an aggressive proposal. (expressed our opposition to) How did the patient **react to** the drug? (respond to, behave on being given)
REMIND	**Remind me about** that tomorrow, will you? (Bring it to my attention.) He **reminds me of** my uncle. (makes me remember)
BE RESPONSIBLE	He's **responsible to** his boss **for** what takes place. (His boss will hold him responsible; he **is responsible for** his actions.) He **is responsible for** the children.
RESULT	The explosion **resulted from** insufficient care being taken of the boilers. (was caused by) Their carelessness **resulted in** the explosion. (caused)
TROUBLE	I shouldn't **trouble about** it. (bother) He's **troubled with** asthma. (suffers from) I **took a lot of trouble over** it. (was careful to do it well) He could **make trouble for you with** your boss. (cause you trouble, cause your boss to be annoyed with you)

Index to Exercises